# Discipline and the Classroom Community: Recapturing Control of Our Schools

Ambrose P. Panico

**Stylex Publishing Co., Inc.**
529 East Maple Lane
Mequon, WI 53092
Phone: (414) 241-8347
Fax: (414) 241-8348
Email: stylex@execpc.com
Web: http://www.execpc.com/stylex

Copyright ©1999 by **Stylex Publishing Co., Inc.**
First Printing

Printed in the United States of America

Title: **Discipline and the Classroom Community: Recapturing Control of Our Schools**
*ISBN 1-878016-18-0*

Includes Illustrations, Graphics, References, Appendices, Forms, Software

Available from:

> **Stylex Publishing Co., Inc.**
> 529 East Maple Lane
> Mequon, WI 53092 USA
> Phone: (414) 241-8347
> Fax: (414) 241-8347
> Email: stylex@execpc.com
> Web: http://www.execpc.com/stylex

All rights reserved. No parts of this book may be reproduced in any form whatsoever, by photograph, mimeograph, computerized scanning, photocopying, production of overhead transparencies, production of slides, or by any other means, by broadcast or transmission via modem, airwaves, or closed circuit, by translation into any kind of language, or by recording electronically or otherwise, without permission in writing from the publisher, Stylex Publishing Co., Inc., except by reviewers, who may quote brief passages in critical articles and reviews.

Production of overhead transparencies, slides, charts, or any video reproduction of any part of this book is prohibited except by previous permission from Stylex. Such permission is often available upon classroom adoption. Stylex Publishing Company makes available many transparency masters for university, college, and training usage.

Text Editing
  Deborah L. Kaiser and Jeffrey S. Kaiser

Layout and Design
  Jeffrey S. Kaiser

Graphics sources:

  Images and graphics protected by copyright as follows:

  ClickArt® Incredible 65,000 Image Pak; © 1996, T/maker Company, a wholly-owned subsidiary of Broderbund Software, Inc. All rights reserved. Used by Permission. Incredible 65,000 Image Pak, ClickArt and T/Maker are registered trademarks of T/Maker Company. Broderbund is a registered trademark of Broderbund Software, Inc.

  Microsoft Corporation © and ®1996.

  New Vision Technologies Inc., All Rights Reserved.

  Stylex Publishing Co., Inc., © 1998, All Rights Reserved

Dedication . . .

*To Ambrose and Mary Panico for teaching me the lessons I really needed to know.*

A sincere thank you. . .

*To Sue Gonzalez and Robin Hanses for your good work in preparing the manuscript. I look forward to using the book for my staff development work. It will make things much easier.*

# Preface

I first heard of Ambrose Panico's work from a graduate student in a course I teach in educational administration. She told me that his work had changed her school from a discipline problem-infested school to a school with the kind of values most new teachers can only dream of and of which other teachers can only reminisce.

This seemed impossible to me. I feared that the myriad of problems affecting our classrooms at the turn of the century could never be overcome without outside intervention into local schools. I blamed parents, a too liberal society, and lawyers for ruining the ability to teach. I knew of too many cases where schools had been forced to operate in such a way as to allow students to hurt their own learning. I knew of parents suing schools and teachers for supposedly depriving their children of civil rights. I knew of administrators who no longer dared to enforce old discipline standards for fear of losing their own jobs. I knew of teachers who had given up sending students down to the office because the student would appear back in their classrooms with grins on their faces within in a few minutes. I saw everyone giving up. I saw everyone blaming educators.

Ambrose Panico's work has given us a way out. It provides us with abilities, for the first time, to practice what we have long been preaching. Without any esoteric or erudite phraseology, and without the espousing of any new bandwagon approaches to ancient problems, *The Classroom Community* provides a stepwise procedure for giving our students the ability to solve their own personal and social problems.

There have long been three major philosophies of discipline in America's schools. One philosophy has fewer fans than ever before, but is worth a mention. It is that which promises that students grow best when left to learn without adult intervention. Memories of Auntie Mame's nephew come to mind -- a laissez faire environment to allow for maximum internal growth, a flowering from within.

A second philosophy is that teachers ought to allow for individual differences in student behavior, but only within boundaries of acceptability set by the adult world. Children can be different, but only to a specified extent. This philosophy is often referred to as boundary maintenance. There has long been an American tradition in elementary schools to use boundary maintenance, the teaching of values, and teacher-student planning to prevent misbehavior. An over-reliance on punishment has not been part of this tradition.

A third major philosophy is best described by the continuous intervention of adults through behavior modification. This includes the use of rewards and punishments as the predominant discipline intervention. High schools, middle schools, and junior high schools have tended toward such a philosophy for many decades. The uses of detention, suspension, and expulsion are more certain examples of punishment used to deter misbehavior. Behavior modification is also the predominant philosophy in the work of special educators who work with emotionally disturbed and behaviorally disordered children.

The three philosophies can easily be placed onto a continuum with a laissez-faire philosophy on one end and behavior modification on the other. Boundary maintenance fits somewhere in the middle.

None of the three philosophies give students the intellectual tools to cure their own problems. Laissez-faire gives almost no guidance whatsoever, boundary maintenance allows only for teacher-student discussion and student involvement in situational rule making, and behavior modification is largely adult-driven regulation. The result of all three traditional approaches to these philosophies is that students learn only to follow rules approved by others for specific situations.

Students have never been given a mechanism to continuously develop themselves as members of a classroom society, a school society, or a community society. They have learned that they can get in trouble when running through a crowded school hallway and not get in trouble for running down a crowded city sidewalk. What they have not learned is why they should not run in areas crowded with people. They have never heard a rule for that. Some have never learned how to be members of any kind of community. They have never learned the many benefits of responsibility in a community context.

Ambrose's years of experience as a principal of an alternative high school near Chicago provides the groundwork and step-by-step procedures for establishing a classroom and school environment rid of severe discipline problems. What is fascinating is that once kids learn how to do it, they do it themselves. That kids from the worst environments can thrive in this milieu gives testimony to its viability. That kids from the best environments increasingly need these skills, gives testimony to its urgency.

Ambrose Panico is Manager of Behavior Disorders, Emotional Disorders, and Safe School Programs for the ECHO Joint Agreement in Illinois. He provides staff development and consulting to schools and organizations intent on reconnecting troubled youth to their schools and communities. Ambrose has been a long-time principal of Pace High School, an award-winning alternative school near Chicago.

Jeffrey S. Kaiser, Ph.D.

# HOW TO USE THE BOOK

This book was written with the practicing teacher in mind. A conscious effort was made to reduce theoretical constructs to either general principles intended to guide the teacher's thinking or actual lessons and activities to simplify the teacher's planning. Chapter One, *Program Overview,* presents the big picture. It explains the *Classroom Community Model* in its entirety. It also previews the individual program components. Chapter Two, *Principles, Perceptions and Methods* provide both a philosophical posture and methods that support the philosophical posture. It is useful for the reader to keep specific students in mind while reading the principles, perceptions, and methods presented in chapter two.

Chapter Three through Chapter Eleven are all structured alike. Chapters begin with a list of student outcomes. Student outcomes are followed by information for teachers with all the background information necessary to teach the chapter's lessons.

Daily lesson plans are provided. Each daily lesson is divided into sections entitled *Preparation Required, Materials Needed* and *Lesson Directions.* The materials are provided at the end of the chapter. Lesson Directions provides a step by step lesson plan. The plan includes the teacher's presentation, student activities and suggested processing prompts. These chapters are followed by *Extending Activities* that allow the teacher to provide additional practice or enrichment.

The book also includes several helpful Appendixes. Appendix A*: Additional Teacher tools*, Appendix B: *Assessments* Appendix C: *Public Relations*, and Appendix D: *Classroom Displays That Promote Community Concepts.*

The reader is encouraged to read the entire book before starting implementation. This will give the reader a broad perspective with which to interface and interpret specific student outcomes, individual model components, and daily lessons. The teacher need not reread chapters one and two. Instead simply read chapters three through eleven in preparation for lesson implementation.

# CONTENTS

*Dedication and Appreciation* ---------------------------------- iv
*Preface* ------------------------------------------------------- v
*How to Use the Book* ------------------------------------------ vii

## CHAPTERS

    I  Program Overview ---------------------------------- 1
   II  Principles, Perceptions, and Methods --------------- 9
  III  The Foundation: Getting to Know Each Other ------ 19
  IV  The Classroom Community Model ------------------- 35
   V  Contracts ------------------------------------------ 47
  VI  Motivation and Basic Needs ------------------------ 69
 VII  Communication Skills ------------------------------ 85
VIII  Outcomes ----------------------------------------- 101
  IX  Community Meetings ------------------------------ 109
   X  Goals --------------------------------------------- 121
  XI  Responsibility Plans ------------------------------- 131

## APPENDICES

  A  Additional Teacher Tools ----------------------------- 149
  B  Assessments ---------------------------------------- 163
  C  Public Relations ------------------------------------- 179
  D  Classroom Displays that Promote Community
      Concepts ------------------------------------------ 183

## REFERENCES ---------------------------------------------- 191

# Chapter I
# PROGRAM OVERVIEW

> *The really important lessons - you teach by example. Demonstrate respect for your students by doing everything you can to position them for success.*

## Factors For Success

Change the climate and change the behavior. Often, the first thing we do when faced with a difficult student or a challenging class is to go down our short list of what's wrong with the student, the class, and certainly the principal for ever putting this group of kids together. Sometimes, we expand our thinking to include the parents and the community. After carefully assigning the student, the class, etc. the appropriate malady or maladies (often they have several), we go about our teacher business of figuring out what they need to do to get better and what we need to do to them to make them feel bad enough to want to get better. How ridiculous! People who feel bad, do badly. In a Classroom Community, the teacher and the community look for ways to help a child (a community member) feel better in order that they might do better. How many times have you made a conscious decision to do something to make yourself feel better so that you can effectively deal with the job at hand? Have you ever gone shopping when your pocketbook says no, because that new outfit is the lift you need to get back on track? As adults, we instinctively understand that in order to do our best we must feel our best. The Classroom Community Teacher works hard to create a classroom climate that helps kids feel good about themselves, their classmates, their teacher, and ultimately their Classroom Community.

> *I've come to a frightening conclusion that I am the DECISIVE ELEMENT in the classroom. It's my personal approach that creates the climate. It's my daily mood that makes the weather. As a teacher, I possess a tremendous power to make a child's life miserable or joyous. I can be a tool of torture or an instrument of inspiration. I can humiliate or humor, hurt or heal. In all situations, it is my response that decides whether a crisis will be escalated or de-escalated and a child humanized or dehumanized.*
> -Haim Ginott (1972)-

While it is beyond the scope of this book to enumerate the principles of sound instructional planning, curriculum design, and delivery, their importance to the functioning of the Classroom Community is too significant to go without mentioning. In an environment where the group's reason to exist is to teach and to learn, how can anyone be happy when this process breaks down? If a classroom is to be a Classroom Community, then all learners must have the benefit of appropriate instruction, appropriate in terms of difficulty, preferred style of learning, and methodology of delivery. Attention must also be paid to variety of activity. How many times have you fought off sleep as the professor drones on? Have you ever participated in classes or workshops where the instructors had obviously thoughtfully planned how much time you spent listening to lectures, watching videos, participating in cooperative learning groups, and completing individual assignments? Possibly those instructors presented instruction that addressed the classes' individual learning styles and, whenever they could, delivered their message in a multi-modal manner. If you are like me, you not only learned more in the second kind of situation, but you enjoyed yourself more. Maybe you appreciated the consideration and respect your instructors accorded you. If you did, make sure you provide your students with the same consideration; it goes a long way toward building a relationship of mutual respect. It greatly limits the inappropriate behavior that is the result of a child's frustrated attempts to master the surrounding environment. How many of us would report to work every day if we were found to be incompetent? As adults, we would seek other employment. Adults have options. Children have compulsory education.

## Classroom Community Definition

A Classroom Community is a classroom where children feel loved. Without meeting and knowing you, it is impossible for me to tell you much, if anything, about yourself. However, I think it safe to assume that you did not become a teacher to get rich. You became a teacher because you loved children. Never forget this. Love is where your power lies. If you succeed in fashioning a community that tells kids and shows kids that they are loved, everything else becomes easier. If you want to discipline a difficult child, you must first nurture them. A Classroom Community is a social organization that values the development and nurturance of relationships. Because the teacher understands the importance of relationships, activities are planned that allow students to get to know each other, trust each other, and serve as support systems for one another. Interactions are based on mutual respect and solidarity of purpose. Community members acknowledge shared values while celebrating individual and cultural differences. Community members establish contracts by which the community can function in a manner that facilitates individual and group goal attainment in a cooperative setting.

In a Classroom Community, learner outcomes include more than learning to read, write, and do arithmetic better than one's classmates. Students learn to accept individual and social responsibility, to be self disciplined, to make difficult decisions, to practice nonviolent conflict resolution, and to help others do the same. Classroom Community members acknowledge the social condition; my right is your responsibility - your right is mine, and then conduct themselves accordingly.

Community members ultimately accept a good degree of responsibility for individual and community outcomes. They are led to the realization that, collectively, they are responsible for creating a school year full of learning and fun. The teacher in a Classroom Community views discipline as a subject area, similar to math, science, social studies, and language arts. This means the teacher accepts the responsibility of planning and teaching discipline lessons. The teacher understands that unless time is designated for establishing a Classroom Community, an inordinate amount will be spent in dealing with disruptive behavior. Discipline is then taught, not levied. Charney (1993) tells us that, "The word discipline is derived from the Latin word *disciplina*, meaning learning. It needs to be associated with positive acts and feats of learning, rather than negatively associated with punishing." Discipline in the traditional sense – obedience – becomes a by-product instead of a goal. The goal is for community members to become socially conscious, self-disciplined, critical thinkers.

Preparation for responsible citizenship in a democratic society demands no less an effort. The teacher gives up some authoritative power but gains control. The difference in a Classroom Community is that students choose to exercise control instead of needing to be controlled. Since students have been taught decision and problem solving skills, the teacher expects them to apply these skills to the daily rigors and frustrations of community life. It is through this sharing of responsibility that the teacher facilitates the development of responsibility.

Kids behave because not only their teacher expects them to, but because their fellow community members expect them to. In a Classroom Community, the teacher's power to influence responsible behavior is exponentially increased by every student that becomes a community member. The positive collective influence is a real force for the disruptive student to consider. The Classroom Community culture encourages productive, supportive, responsible behavior.

## Classroom Community Components: Implementing the Program

The Classroom Community curriculum is initially taught as is any other instructional unit. The difference with this unit is that once it is taught and practiced, students are expected and encouraged to use their new skills and knowledge to manage their own behavior and to positively influence their fellow community members to manage theirs. The initial instructional phase is covered in approximately thirty class periods (based on a class period of forty-five minutes). The model is best implemented when taught one period a day for thirty consecutive days. Actual implementation time varies based on the unique composition of your class. Once all components have been taught, only one period per week is scheduled for formal Classroom Community work. The work now takes the form of a Classroom Community meeting. Community business and most community problem solving/conflict resolutions are addressed through the Classroom Community weekly meeting. The teacher may also elect to call an additional community meeting any time the need arises. Some teachers start each day with a 5-10 minute check-in meeting. The Classroom Community Curriculum is made up of the following components or instructional units: the foundation, the model, contracts, motivation and basic needs, communication skills, outcomes, meetings, goals, and responsibility plans. Components should be presented in this order.

In order for the reader to better comprehend the whole curriculum, an individual component description and suggested implementation schedule is provided. Subsequent chapters are devoted to more complete component descriptions and the concomitant lesson plans and activities required for easy implementation.

## Component Overview and Implementation

## Foundation Component

People -- including children -- work better, more effectively and more harmoniously with people they know and like. If you do not believe me, ask yourself why corporate America spends millions of dollars every year to send top management and key project teams on retreats. Put the book down and take a minute to think about your best boss (this could be a principal, a department chair, a grade level lead teacher, etc.). By "best boss," I mean the person who empowered you to be your best. Is the person you have in mind necessarily your smartest boss, most efficient boss, and most cutting edge boss? Or are you thinking of a boss who valued and nurtured a relationship with you, a relationship based on mutual respect? A boss who empowered you to follow your passions? Who provided you choices? Who made sure you had important work? Relationships will have a lot to do with everything that either happens or fails to happen in your community. The Foundation Component is a series of experiential education and get-to-know-each-other activities designed to 1) speed up the natural process of becoming comfortable with new people, 2) direct the process so that everyone gets to know everyone else, avoiding the formation of counter-productive cliques, 3) lay groundwork for the acceptance and celebration of individual and cultural differences and, 4) begin to create a climate of trust so that positive risk-taking behavior and problem solving can occur.

Instructional time is approximately five (5) class periods. Remember that relationship building leads into relationship maintenance. Nurture relationships in your community on a regular basis and spend as much time as possible doing so during the first four to six weeks of the year. It will be time well spent. If things start to break down, it is probably time to focus on relationships. Often times, this is best accomplished by providing experiential education activities designed to enhance group solidarity. When things break down, it is usually best not to talk or lecture, but simply do. Do something productive together, celebrate your success, then talk.

## Model Component.

Consideration for your students as responsible learners starts here. Rather than having your students guessing, or worse yet, thinking you've finally lost it, tell them what's going on and why. You introduce the Classroom Community Model to your students and, in the process, ask them if they prefer to spend roughly 180 days (1080 hours) in a traditional classroom or in a Classroom Community. You challenge them to step up to the plate and accept responsibility for what the year will bring. You convince them that this time it is not business as usual. You empower them by expecting them to take control. Instructional time is approximately two (2) class periods.

## Communication Skills Component

In order to function in any group, but especially in a group like a Classroom Community, where you are expected to make sound decisions and solve conflicts, communication skills are a necessity. Too often, we put our students in situations of application without ever teaching them the prerequisite skills necessary for success. In many of my workshops, someone will say, "they don't have any social skills, I can't put them in groups," and someone else replies, "that's why you have to put them in groups." I finish the round off by saying something like, "let's put them in groups to teach them social skills." I get to do this because I am the workshop leader. In a Classroom Community, we ask our students to participate in regularly scheduled and as needed community meetings, but first, we must teach them some basic communication skills. Skills include 1) active listening, 2) managing conversation traffic, 3) using "I" messages, 4) understanding and respecting individual perspectives, 5) identifying mutual interest and win-win situations, and other skills as individual community members or the community at large needs them. Instructional time is approximately five (5) class periods. Basic communication skills are taught before community meetings are attempted.

## Motivation and Basic Needs Component

In this component, students are taught about the basic physiological and psychological needs that drive human behavior. Students are helped to evaluate how they are meeting their needs and, where necessary, taught more socially acceptable methods of need gratification. The community works to find socially acceptable avenues for students to meet their psychological needs. Instructional time is approximately two (2) class periods. While most physiological needs are addressed outside of the school building, psychological needs to a large degree are addressed during the school day. An understanding of the relationship between the basic psychological needs and the behaviors they drive empowers students to analyze their actions more effectively and ultimately change their own behavior.

## Goals Component

In this unit, students are asked to reflect on their goals for the school year. They are taught to set goals and to identify activities and behaviors likely to support goal attainment. Individual and Community goals are written. Instructional time is approximately two (2) class periods. Most students will not have established goals and will be somewhat surprised that they are being asked to do so. They view the setting of goals as something adults (teacher/parents) do for them. Individual and community goals will serve as behavioral benchmarks for disruptive, off-task students.

## Outcomes Component

In order to manage one's behavior, one must first understand the cause and effect relationship. Understanding this relationship is the first step to predicting outcomes and eventually controlling them. In the Classroom Community, students are allowed and encouraged to make decisions and to accept their outcomes, positive and negative. Students engage in self-evaluation and, over a period of time, develop an internal locus of control. Students with an internal locus of control believe that they create their own outcomes. Students also learn about different types of outcomes so that they can use their knowledge of outcomes when writing Responsibility Plans. Instructional time is approximately two (2) class periods. The chapter on outcomes emphasizes the importance of exposing your students to instructional or constructive outcomes. Young people tend to be very punitive when initially empowered to develop outcomes. Please note that the word "outcomes" in used instead of the more generally accepted "consequences" because of the negative connotation often associated with the latter. Using the term "outcomes" facilitates the development of an internal locus of control. It helps students accept responsibility and ownership of their positive and negative behaviors.

## Community Meetings Component

Students are taught to participate in two types of community meetings. The first type is the Community Business Model. This meeting is used for agenda items, such as planning the culminating activity for an instructional unit, planning a field trip, planning a party, drafting a menu for free time activities, selecting a class pet, etc. The second type is the Conflict Resolution/Problem Solving Model. The Conflict Resolution/Problem Solving Model is used to solve community issues as well as conflicts between individual community members. All members of the community (teachers and students) recommend items for the community meeting agenda. Instructional time is approximately three (3) class periods. The Community meeting provides a vehicle for students to test and practice communication, decision making, and problem solving skills. More than anywhere else, it is here that shared responsibility becomes a reality. Teachers and students share the responsibility of conducting community affairs and solving community conflicts.

## Contracts Component

Students are actively involved in the writing of Classroom Community contracts. These contracts are agreements made between community members about what the community values, about the basic rights and responsibilities of individuals, about the rules required to support the values and rights established, and about outcomes for adhering to or failing to adhere to classroom community rules. Instructional time is approximately five (5) class periods. The teacher is reminded that sometimes the process is more important than the product. This is truly the case when writing Classroom Community Contracts. Students must feel that they have ownership of their Community Contracts. Contracts serve as behavioral benchmarks for disruptive off-task students.

## Responsibility Plan Component

A Responsibility Plan is an individual plan a student writes when an irresponsible behavior is either significant in nature or frequency. The Responsibility Plan helps the student to self-evaluate. It asks the student to describe the behavior and identify the basic need motivating it. The Responsibility Plan facilitates students interfacing their behavior with their individual goals, and the Community Contracts. It affirms that students are responsible for their own behavior and the effect that behavior may have on other community members. It encourages the development of an internal locus of control. The student ultimately must develop a plan to do better. Instructional time is approximately two (2) class periods. Students learn the mechanics of writing Responsibility Plans quickly. The ability to apply the skill to their own emotionally charged situations develops over time.

# Chapter II

# PRINCIPLES, PERCEPTIONS, AND METHODS

> *Respect your students by refraining from doing anything to them you would not want done to you, by refusing to do for them anything they can do for themselves, and by empowering them to do the things they think they cannot do.*

While this is certainly a "how to" book, I have too much respect for teachers and too much concern for their students to ever presume that any recipe I could furnish would supersede an individual teacher making an individual decision regarding an individual student. I believe that canned discipline programs do this. They take the teacher and the heart and soul of the classroom out of the process. How foolish! Rather than provide a one, two, three step hierarchy of consequences to be administered blindly to all students across all situations, I choose to provide some guiding principles for your prescriptive application. I ask that you read them carefully and consider them thoughtfully. I hope you will read them with particular students and situations in mind. The principles I share with you have served me well. They have allowed me to work effectively with all types of students in many different settings. If you find yourself ready to initiate an interaction with a student that violates one or more of these principles, consider your actions again. Make sure that yours is not a reaction. Rethink the situation and see if you can come up with another plan. If, after careful analysis, your initial plan of interaction still seems the best way to go, act on it. Remember to evaluate its effectiveness as you go.

## Principles

Teaching discipline and helping students to handle their behavior is an important part of teaching. Control and prevention of disruptive behavior is the by-product, not the primary goal, of a sound discipline program. As already stated, the primary goal is to help students to become self-disciplined. Accept the responsibility of planning and implementing discipline lessons. These may be the most important lessons you will teach your students.

All interactions with students, including those that occur as a result of behavior problems, must preserve the student's dignity. The effects of any interaction/intervention on the student - teacher relationship should always be considered. Remember that you will see and work with this student tomorrow. Your ability to serve as an agent for change, as a teacher, is dependent upon your ability to maintain the relationship. If at all possible, serious disciplinary interventions should be carried out in private. Not only do you have a much better chance of reaching a positive outcome by eliminating the "face saving" dynamic but also you demonstrate your commitment to preserving your student's dignity. Teachers do not always have the option of a private conference. Teachers always have the responsibility of preserving their students' dignity. This means you simply refrain from doing anything to your student that you would not want done to you.

Most learning occurs through modeling. If you want kids to treat each other with respect, treat the kids with respect. If you want the kids to give each other the benefit of the doubt, give the kids the benefit of the doubt. If you want the kids to resolve conflicts calmly, do the same.

There is absolutely no better way to help than to talk. Help kids make connections between emotions and behavior, between behavior and outcomes, between values and a life that supports those values. Work hard to understand the students' world views. Do they believe the world is fair? Do they find school a comfort zone or a hostile environment? Do they see adults as kind and caring or abusive and selfish? Do they believe themselves competent or inept? The students' worldviews are all important to their motivation and ability to change. For lasting change to occur, there must be a change in the class' worldview. If the students' world views include an image of school as a place where they really do not belong, a place where they are considered inept, motivation and control will necessarily be required from external sources. It is only when the child's world view changes and school is considered a place of comfort and competency that motivation and control begins to come from within.

View problem behaviors and crisis situations as teaching moments. View your role not as a consequence-giver but as a problem-solver. When working with a difficult, at-risk, or troubled child, it represents a chance for the teacher to focus on an area of deficit. If the child has a serious problem, the problem will present itself again and again. Rather than view it as a repeated interruption to learning, you must view it as the child's request for you to teach them what they need to know most. Crisis situations provide an opportunity for cognitive reorganization. This means the adult must talk with the child.

Have a plan when you sit down to help a student work through a problem. Most good interview techniques include 1) allowing the students some time and space to calm down, 2) helping the students to articulate their perceptions of what happened, 3) facilitating the students' matching their perceptions to reality, 4) encouraging the students to identify decision points and ultimately accept responsibility for their parts in the situation, and 5) developing a plan for solving the current problem and for handling similar situations more productively in the future. Life Space Intervention is a therapeutic interview technique for working with a student in crisis (Wood and Long 1991). The technique is very compatible with the Classroom Community Model.

Self-esteem is the foundation upon which all else is built. If students have problems that are left unresolved, they deduct a measure of self-esteem from their self-esteem bank. If they have problems and you help resolve them, they make a deposit in their self-esteem bank. If you let them file bankruptcy, you are all in for a long year. If, on a regular basis, you help them solve problems within the context of your Classroom Community, the students will accept negative outcomes while preserving their relationships with you and the community. A problem that is brought full circle to solution ceases to be a problem. In many ways, it is a challenge met and conquered. Done correctly, it facilitates the development of an internal locus of control.

Instructional outcomes do more than just stop irresponsible behavior; they provide options and teach more productive behaviors. This type of outcome is referred to as an "instructional outcome" and is discussed more completely in the chapter on outcomes. Sound outcomes do not demean a child; instead, they increase self-confidence and foster the development of an internal locus of control.

There are two ways to keep order; one is through fear and the other is by providing the individuals involved with a stake in the situation. Truly tough kids do not respond to fear or obedience-based discipline models. Life has already done more to them than you would legally or morally ever consider doing. They see no reason in and of itself to obey. Obviously, you must provide them with a stake in the situation. The Classroom Community does this.

Positive Collective Influence can be a potent tool. Share the power with your students. Too often, we ask and expect our students to accept responsibility without providing them the necessary information. Let them know that you do not and can not completely control what they do. Be honest and explain that while you have control over some things that allow you to have influence on students (i.e. grades, privileges, etc.), you cannot really make a student do something the student will not do. Explain that each member of the community has influence and that really good communities are communities where members pool their influence to make sure that what is important to the community is actually accomplished. Work on developing Positive Collective Influence. Make sure to communicate to your students that your desire to empower them does not mean that you would ever abdicate your responsibility to make sure of everyone's physical and psychological safety.

Empower your students! Analyze your interactions with your students. Ask yourself, *"will this interaction support or diminish my students' perception of themselves as capable, competent, 'I can' individuals? Will this interaction increase or diminish my students' perceptions of themselves as contributors to our community? As someone with something to bring to the table?"* Ask yourself, *"will this interaction help or hurt my relationship with my student?"* Act accordingly.

Always evaluate both the immediate and long-term effects of your actions. Remember that an interaction that may prove to be expedient may also prove to be counter-productive to long range goals. It may be easy to demand obedience, especially from those students who allow you to do so, but it may also rob them of an opportunity to self-evaluate, stifle any meaningful relationship building between you and the student, sow the seeds of resentment, increase the possibility of passive-aggressive behavior, and inadvertently model "bully" type behavior for the rest of your class.

Self-evaluation is a necessary process for the development of an internal locus of control. Provide your students ample opportunities to engage in self-evaluation. Opportunities should be provided in social, behavioral, and academic contexts.

Remember that in all situations you do not do your students a service when you keep them dependent upon you. This must not be misconstrued to mean that you should not help your students. You simply must restrict yourself from taking work that is rightfully theirs. Help only as much as you are needed. An independent effort that falls short of perfection is much better than a perfect product that falls short of demanding a meaningful effort. This holds true in behavioral and academic tasks.

When dealing with serious behaviors and disruptions, treat every student and every situation on an individual basis. Before deciding how much help to provide, consider the student's social and emotional maturity level, intellectual functioning, current emotional state, outside stressors, and any other factors your "gut" tells you are important. Help the student establish a reasonable goal or outcome and then provide as much support as you feel necessary to help the student succeed.

Develop and regularly visit behavior benchmarks. A behavior benchmark is any artifact that, once in place, can be used to remind students that their behavior is in conflict with their declared values, stated goals, and/or Community Contracts. A behavior benchmark could be Classroom Community Contracts, or individual goals that students set for themselves. Mal-adaptive behavior is interfaced with behavior benchmarks as part of the self-evaluation process. Visit your behavior benchmarks often and you will help your students develop internal compasses to navigate the rest of their lives.

Think of discipline related interactions as occurring simultaneously on three different levels. Consider what you can do on each of the three levels. If you are like most teachers, you will have given careful thought to the Prevention Level, and you already will have implemented most of what I enumerate. You will have been forced to develop some sort of plan for the Intervention Level; however, it may be conventional (punitive) in nature. If you have done much on the Teaching Level, congratulations! You are way ahead of the game. It is work on this level that will produce opportunities for your students to become self-disciplined individuals. Prevention is anything the teacher or community does to prevent discipline problems from occurring. This includes communication of expectations, communication of consequences, establishment of community contracts, providing varied ways for students to meet their basic needs, attention to learning difficulties, becoming knowledgeable about individual student differences, becoming knowledgeable about different techniques and theories, and developing and nurturing supportive teacher-student and student-student relationships.

Teaching is anything the teacher or community does to provide its members with information and skills that allow them to meet their basic psychological needs while interacting with the rest of the school community in both an age appropriate and socially responsible manner. This includes:

- exposure to basic information on human behavior
- communication skills
- decision making skills
- anger/frustration management

The adage of "Teach when teachable" is applicable to this level. The idea is that students are only available to learn these skills and accept this knowledge when they are not upset or emotionally charged. If students are taught a skill such as anger management when they are not angry, there is a good chance that, with cueing, they will be able to apply it when they become angry. In the Classroom Community model, both the teaching and the application of the skill to real life situations are considered integral parts of the discipline program.

Intervention is anything the teacher or community does after a discipline problem occurs. This includes:

- conferences
- facilitation of alternative behavior selection
- negative outcomes
- individual responsibility plans
- community meetings
- time out
- when necessary, removal from class or school

Do not confuse a lack of motivation with a lack of discipline. Meaningful curriculum and interesting instruction are the best preventive discipline methods available. Too much unstructured time almost always leads to problem behavior. For academically depressed students, remedial instruction is a must. All the self-concept building in the world can not fool a student who is unable to read.

Do not grade Classroom Community activities. Honest participation is your real goal. Consider the following ideas for academic grading:

- Make sure to communicate how you will grade and what percentage of the grade will be based on homework, participation, quizzes, tests, projects, etc.
- Remember that this is not college. You teach more than just content. You need to attach points to things like homework and participation.
- Regular feedback is very important.
- Facilitate your students keeping track of their own grades. In this way, even your grading system fosters an internal locus of control.

When interacting with a student who is growing up in an economically and socially disadvantaged community or dysfunctional home, it is very important never to discount the child's reality. Instead, acknowledge the situation, help the child cope with it, and when necessary, explain that behaviors that may be acceptable and even adaptive at home or in the community may not be acceptable or adaptive in school. You are now in a position to teach behaviors that are adaptive in school.

# Perceptions

Underlying every manipulative demand is a legitimate request to meet a basic human need.

Teachers must once again give themselves permission to love and care for their students with no strings attached. Teachers who believe they should care for their students without expecting or needing the children to reciprocate live longer. Teachers must realize that nurturance and attention are as basic to children thriving as are food and water. It is immoral and simply not effective to withhold them as part of some sort of reinforcement paradigm. The teacher who wishes to discipline an at-risk student must first nurture that student. Teachers must remind themselves that we all need to feel safe, competent, and connected to other human beings. The student is probably trying to meet those needs (Maslow 1954). Teachers must believe that underlying every manipulative demand is a legitimate request to meet a basic human need. They must invest in helping their students to find productive, socially responsible ways to meet their needs.

Hope must live in the classroom. Teachers must believe in their ability to make a difference. This allows them to invest in change and to work with all children. At-risk children must believe that things can be different, that things can be better, and that they can be successful students. Children must believe in their teacher and ultimately believe in themselves. It is much easier for at-risk students to believe things can be different in a Classroom Community setting, because instead of just being punished for not behaving, they, along with their classmates, are taught how to behave. For the first time, the school's curriculum actually addresses the skills and competencies they need most. The Classroom Community model not only actively teaches discipline but also provides students daily opportunities to use skills they have learned to solve community and individual student problems. The at-risk or included special education student is no less a community member than the honor student. The honor student may need accelerated math while the at-risk student needs accelerated communication skills. Both are taught in the Classroom Community. Both students must learn to accept and support the other. Students are helped to understand that, because they are classmates, one's behavior has a positive or negative effect on the others. They begin to see that one's right is the others' responsibility. Most discipline issues are resolved by the community in the community. Students are provided the information and skills to solve these issues and encouraged to take the responsibility for doing so.

Teachers must understand that their relationships with their students are central to all that either happens or fails to happen in their classrooms. For most students, the teacher assumes the role of substitute parent and the child assigns to them the attributes and qualities they know their parents to have. If students have experienced good parenting, the teacher benefits greatly. If they have received poor parenting or been neglected or abused, the teacher starts at a significant disadvantage. The teacher must be willing to meet students where they are and work from that point forward.

Teachers must understand that what children believe about themselves is more important in determining behavior than is any list of objective facts about them. What children believe about the adults charged with their care runs a close second. Your students will form their opinion of you within the first six weeks of the year, and it will probably not change, even if you do. You must make bonding and relationship building a primary goal at the start of the year. At-risk, difficult students will probably not give you a second chance.

Teachers must be creative thinkers. Teachers who are creative thinkers are always willing to try anything that might help a student. They never, ever say "That's the way I've always done it in my classroom." The chances for success with difficult students increase with this "try anything" type of thinking, as possibilities are limited only by creativity. Teachers who are creative thinkers usually expand their personal creativity by involving colleagues in their search for solutions.

Teachers must be risk takers. They must be willing to make mistakes and learn from them. Like professional athletes, teachers should remember and enjoy the day's success and dismiss the day's failures. This type of attitude builds energy for tomorrow's challenges. On a good day, a good teacher probably breaks even with a difficult kid.

Teachers must not allow themselves to burn precious psychological energy on negative, self-defeating thoughts. They must acknowledge that teaching has gotten more difficult. Teachers must realize that we are easy targets for all of society's ills, and refuse to accept the blame for conditions beyond our control. The vast majority of teachers work very hard and do a commendable job. I do not feel bad about what teachers have always done and continue to do for children; I do feel terrible about the living conditions we as a society allow so many children to endure. I am careful not to marry these two perceptions, as that would damage my self-image and diminish my effectiveness as a teacher. Take pride in our profession.

Teachers must allow themselves to slow down and enjoy their students. The amount of things for which we have become responsible can be exhausting. The constant push for accountability is stressful, so keep things in perspective. Be responsible, but set your own priorities, as only you know what your kids need.

Please take the time to laugh with your students. Teachers who find humor in their classrooms and especially in their own foolish behavior and mistakes feel better about teaching.

## Methods

Do what's right for your students. You know what that is, and you know how to do it.

Cooperative Learning is an extremely compatible instructional methodology for the Classroom Community or any other shared responsibility based discipline model. Having students work in diads, triads, and small groups leads to the development of relationships and provides an opportunity for students to apply their Classroom Community communication skills. Cooperative learning maximizes cooperation and minimizes competition. Consider using Cooperative learning lessons for part of your instruction program.

Journal Writing or *Journaling* is a good way to have your student process daily life in the Classroom Community. Provide time every day for students to make entries in their Journals. They can write about things that happen in the community, and things they plan on doing. They can express their feelings and vent their frustrations. They can do drawings, write poems, and craft stories. The teacher can also provide additional structure by making a specific assignment such as: 1) please keep a journal record of how many times you meet your competency needs in the next three days, or 2) please write about the last time you had a conflict and how you handled it. Some sharing of journal work can be fun and is suggested. If journals are confidential, share only with the students' permission.

Mind Mapping, although usually seen in conjunction with a mainstream academic task, is wonderful for dealing with feelings and facilitating problem solving. Example: use a particular problem as your central theme and generate possible feelings. See the exercise "Drive My Behavior" in Chapter 6, *Motivation and Basic Needs* for an example of mind mapping. Use color, special fonts, key words, and catchy sayings to enhance your mind maps. Jensen (1988) tells us that the current mind mapping strategy emerged in the mid 1950's. He suggests having students work in teams to do mind maps.

Classroom Community Conversation Boards can be used as a regular vehicle for having students generate conversation to start community meetings. Simply designate a specific area and put up a large piece of paper (roll paper or newsprint) with one line of writing. Make sure you have a marker or two available and let the kids go. Example: Our Community Means _____. Students can finish the prompt with their individual answers. See Community Conversation Boards, Extending Activities, in Chapter 3: Foundation.

Role play as much as time allows. Role playing works well for practicing a skill a student wants to use in a particular situation. Example: John would like to negotiate a bigger allowance with his father. Role-play also works well as a reality check for determining how realistic a conflict resolution might be. Example: Tyrone says that he will simply ignore Sam if Sam continues to talk about Tyrone's girl friend. Role play the situation within the safety of the community and see what happens. If Tyrone needs suggestions and/or support the community is there to provide it. Consider the use of props in your role playing; the kids love to use them. It also makes the role playing more realistic. Some teachers create a prop box stocked with items often used in their role plays. Consider using the Role Play situation sheet provided in Appendix A.

Discussion is always good. Students learn from each other when you provide structured opportunities for them to talk and exchange ideas. Use the discussion challenge sheet provided in Appendix A.

Identify specific skills that individuals or the community need to live by their community contracts. Have your students work in small groups to identify five that will help them support the values their contracts expound. Consider specific skills when helping a student write a responsibility plan. Suggest to a student who is writing a Responsibility Plan focussed on staying out of fights that learning to respond to teasing is a skill you could write and that student could learn. Use the Skill-Builder Worksheet you will find in Appendix A.

Several different methods of forming work and problem solving groups are presented throughout the book. In some Preparation Required and Materials Needed sections, the teacher is simply reminded to decide on a method for forming groups, diads, or triads. The teacher should give some thought to both the size and composition of the groups. These are important instructional decisions. Things to consider include:

1. a short period of time usually means a smaller group
2. a need to make sure particular students do not find ways to avoid the experience usually dictates a smaller group
3. a desire to bring the full measure of your students' resources to bear on a specific task might mean a larger group more brains equals more resources
4. students with developed communication and social skills can make large groups extremely productive
5. smaller groups work to increase group member relationship building
6. of course the nature and specificity of the task must always be considered
7. (Johnson, Johnson, and Holubec 1994)

Another consideration for a Classroom Community teacher is making sure that cliques do not form and that all students get to know each other.

Assessment of individual students' behavioral, social, and emotional growth can be achieved through an analysis of the students' Classroom Community activities. While Classroom Community activities themselves should not be given a grade (A, B, C), they can be used as authentic assessments. A special education student's Individual Educational Program (IEP) might list Classroom Community activities and goals. Observations, check lists, work samples, and Responsibility Plans may be used as part of a behavior disordered student's functional behavior analysis.

Peer Mediation is a method of nonviolent conflict resolution that philosophically aligns nicely with the Classroom Community model. A trained student peer mediation cadre best mediates conflicts that occur between members of different classrooms. Train a few students from each classroom who can then serve on such a cadre. The Classroom Community Conflict Resolution/Problem Solving Format is adaptable for this use. However, there are many Peer Mediation Programs complete with mediator training materials available. The Peer Mediation: Conflict Resolution in Schools Program is one program that interfaces well with the Classroom Community model (Crawford, Schrumpf, and Usadel 1991).

# Chapter III

# THE FOUNDATION: GETTING TO KNOW EACH OTHER

*Remember and help America remember that the fellowship of human beings is more important than the fellowship of race and class and gender in a democratic society.*
- Marian Wright Edelman-

## Outcomes

1. Students will get to know and cooperate with one another.
2. Students will develop a basic trust level with each other and develop positive risk taking attitudes.
3. Students will accept their individual differences
4. Students will become familiar with the Experiential Education Format.
5. Students will experience fun and success in-group problem solving situations.

## Teacher Information

The concept of using the environment as teacher is not new but it is too seldom applied in the school setting. The Outward Bound tradition of stress/challenge and experiential education has much to offer educators involved in Responsibility Education programs. The idea of first providing an activity then allowing time for processing seems simple however, in traditional education it is seldom done, unless one considers listening to a lecture or watching a video an activity. Experiential Education recommends that an activity must be of a participatory nature. Kids first do, then they process; play first, talk later. Enjoy the game then figure out the important lessons. Experiential Education provides students continuous opportunities to problem solve while maximizing cooperation and minimizing competition. Individual and group cohesiveness are stressed. Leadership is viewed as fluid and dependent upon individual strengths and situational demands. Kids learn that, in a really productive group, the leader is not always the same person.

As families and communities become increasingly diverse, it is risky to assume that any group of students share a completely common bank of experiences. The worldview (perspective and assumptions) our students use to make sense of and process events varies greatly! It is a faulty assumption that all students have experienced first hand or have witnessed significant adults experiencing "win/win" outcomes through the application of nonviolent conflict resolution skills. It is also unlikely that all students would find an adult who uses non-violent conflict resolution skills to be an adult to emulate. If the student's worldview (perspective) is that of a hostile world, the nonviolent adult may be viewed as just another "punk" or potential victim.

One way teachers can at least be sure that their students have the same experience to process is to provide the experience. Teachers can ask their students to begin the processing phase of the lesson. By holding the experience constant, differences in perspective become clearer and thus easier to work with and through. The processing of common experiences provides a wonderful opportunity for students to develop an understanding of the importance of perspective, the importance of an individual's or a culture's point of view. They learn first-hand that not everyone is the same nor do they think the same. They start to consider the possibility that two people may have the same experience but perceive it differently, think about the experience in totally different ways, and quite possibly reach different but none the less valid conclusions. Students who understand the importance of perspective are more likely to take risks, trust each other, become less inhibited, and ultimately become more accepting of themselves and their follow community members. Most experiential education activities/lessons follow a simple but effective format.

## Experiential Education Activity Format

- Introduce the activity.
- Demonstrate the activity.
- Check for understanding.
- Have the students do the activity.
- Process the activity.
- Celebrate the communities' success/effort.

When demonstrating the activity, the teacher should provide clear, concise directions. Caution must be exercised to confine the directions to the activity, as it is easy to slip into the processing stage of the lesson. When this happens, the teacher may provide the deductions, conclusions, and extrapolations for their students. Obviously, this robs the students of the intended higher level learning experience. The teacher should keep in mind that most experiential education activities are more easily understood when a visual demonstration is provided. Often, the teacher may need to have one or more students help in the demonstration. The demonstration should always be followed by questions to check for understanding. When the teacher is satisfied that the students understand the activity, the students should attempt the activity. In the event the students experience more than desirable difficulty, the activity should be stopped and the teacher should re-teach/demonstrate/or provide additional information. While it is considered healthy that the students experience success or failure based on the group's effort and ability, failure should not be the result of confusion over the mechanics of the activity itself.

The most important and often the least attended to part of any experiential learning lesson is the processing step. This step can be easy to rush through, as it is not as much "fun" as the actual activity itself. Processing can also be difficult to do, as the students have not been educated as to the rationale for doing experiential education. Additionally, the teacher may not be comfortable with the processing step. Students must be provided the opportunity to express their individual thoughts and feelings. If the students fail to make important connections between the learning activity and Classroom Community applications, the teacher must facilitate this outcome. Specific processing questions are provided for all activities, however, some general processing questions include: How were you feeling during the activity? During a particular part of the activity? How do you think your partner or people in different roles felt? Did anyone take a leadership role? Did the leader change? Why? Did anyone feel left out? What made the activity easy? What made it hard? Did people cooperate? What would you do differently? What did you learn about yourself, others, your community? How will what you learned help you, others, your community? Did you have fun?

While the mechanics of teaching are always important, nowhere is your personal approach more important than it is when implementing the Foundation lessons. For many of your students, Experiential Education is new. Anything new causes some anxiety; however, it also generates curiosity and excitement. Your introduction to the activities must generate interest and provide the motivation necessary to capitalize on your students' natural curiosity and propensity to play.

Your enthusiasm will be contagious. Initially, there will be one or two students who will not feel comfortable jumping in and participating actively. These students need to know that "pass" is always an option and that participation can take the form of observation. Naturally, your goal will be to gradually increase the level of participation of these students. This can be accomplished by working privately with a student, often letting them preview the activity and talk it through with you or another student prior to your teaching it to the class. Another option is to ask the student to observe the class activity so that you or a student of their choice can process it with them later. The student can also observe the activity and process it immediately with the class, however, in this case, you want to inform the class of the arrangement before hand. Kids and even adults can get touchy about comments from individuals who did not take part in the activity. My experience has been that, so long as the class knows that they are not being evaluated but instead are helping a fellow community member get comfortable with the process, things go well. Instructional time for this component is approximately five (5) class periods.

# Day One: Student Introductions

## Preparation Required and Materials Needed

One *This Is Me* worksheet per student, states of the USA abbreviations, random pairs matching, two sets of index cards, one of states and one of state abbreviations (see end of this chapter), teacher made.

## Lesson Directions

Form your students into pairs by having half the class select a card from the states cards and half from the capitals cards. Have your pairs sit together. Ask everyone to complete the "This is Me" Worksheet. Tell your students to first choose an animal that they identify with, one that has qualities they like, an animal they would most like to be and to draw a picture of that animal in the picture frame. When they are through drawing, they should answer the animal questions. Next, ask them to list three things about themselves that they are proud of. Ask them to choose three words that end in "ing" that describe them. Next, they are to list three things that they like to do. Finally, they should list three people who they respect, admire, love. They can be family, friends, teachers, classmates, celebrities, anybody. Fifteen minutes is usually sufficient to complete the worksheet. Have students take turns explaining their drawings and answers to their partner. This usually takes a total of ten minutes, five minutes each. Students then take turns introducing their partners to the community. If time is short, you can instruct students to share only their favorite answer per category.

# Day Two: Community Hand Print

## Preparation Required and Materials Needed

Decide on the number of students you will have in each small work group. Depending on the size of your class, choose groups of eight to ten students. Two to four groups work well. Divide your total number of students by the selected group size; i.e., divide 28 by seven and you will have four groups of seven. Have your students count off by 4's (1,2,3,4). Like numbers will be a group. Since you have four groups, you will need four pieces of large newsprint or roll paper. The size of the paper depends on group size and the size of your students' hands. You want paper that is long enough for all students to trace outlines of their hands, both hands along the perimeter of the paper. If you are not sure of how large a piece of paper to provide, provide one larger than needed and trim to size later. Students will trace their hand outlines only along the top and bottom of the paper. The paper's long dimension runs horizontally.

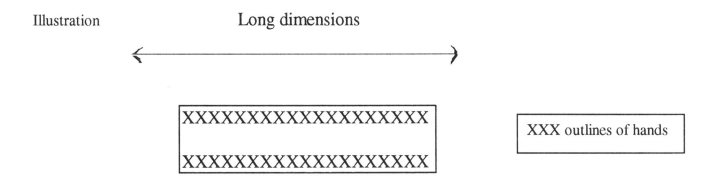

You will also need several different colored markers for each group. This can be a messy activity but it will prove worth the mess. Washable markers are advisable, as students will get some ink on their hands and whatever surface you have them work on.

## Lesson Directions

Tell the groups that you are making a Community Hand Print Banner. Their job is for each community member to draw the outline of both their left and right hands around the perimeter of the top and bottom of their piece of paper. Ideally, each member will draw their outlines once on either the top or bottom of the paper; however, if it does not work out perfectly, somebody can draw an extra outline or two, making sure that they end up with a continuous border. The border covers all but about the first and last two to four inches of paper. After the hand print banner is completed, all members write their first names and one thing about themselves they want to share in their handprints. Any extra handprints may be used for the individual's nickname(s). Groups now join their respective sections with masking tape and/or glue. You will probably notice that your border is incomplete; it needs ends. This is where the teacher's handprints go. Draw outlines of our own hands to complete the ends. You will probably have eight blanks to fill in. Do so with your name, the names of your spouse and children, things you want to share about yourself with your kids (they love to hear your nickname). Hang the banner in a prominent place. Make sure it is low enough for students to reach the top of the banner. They will need to do so for tomorrow's activity. Process with your students: What does the continuous border symbolize? Why do we share about ourselves? Did it help you get to know each other? Do people get along better if they know each other? Did you have fun?

## Day Three Focus: The Community on School

## Preparation Required and Materials Needed

Different colored construction paper (cut the construction paper in half) scissors, pencils, glue.

## Lesson Directions

Have each student trace the outline of just one of their hands on a half sheet of construction paper. Next have the student cut the outline out. The student should print their name and one thing they like about school on the hand. You can have students decorate their hands if you wish. Students take turns going to the banner and introducing themselves to the class. They also share what they like about school, then glue their hand somewhere in the center of the banner. Process with your students: What do you think of our banner? Was it a little uncomfortable getting up in front of the class? Would you like to be a little more comfortable/relaxed? If we were all comfortable with each other how would it affect our year? Was it fun?

## Day Four: Focus on Working Together

## Preparation Required and Materials Needed

Two boxes (approximately 500) drinking straws and a roll of one-inch masking tape per group. Divide your class into groups of around four to six students. Attempt to form heterogeneous groups. Put kids into groups who you think would not ordinarily group themselves together. Have eighteen-inch squares marked off with masking tape, one for each group on a table or section of floor, depending on where they will be working.

## Lesson Directions

Tell the groups their job is to construct the tallest self-standing skyscraper they can. Explain that the base of their skyscraper must fit within the eighteen-inch space you marked off. Tell them they must find ways to insure that everyone participates. Give them about twenty to twenty-five minutes to construct their skyscraper. You will be surprised at the results. Process with your students: Did everyone participate? Does anyone disagree? Did you make a plan or just start in? Did groups who had plans do better? Was it fun?

Leave your skyscrapers on display for a while. It can be fun to connect all the skyscrapers into one structure. This can be done on the horizontal or vertical plane.

Building up is really fun. Ask your school custodian for a tall ladder and some help (it's safer). You can go to the ceiling, but you'll need to attach the skyscraper to it. Masking tape works well for plaster ceilings. A little wire is great for dropped ceilings. See extending activities at the end of the chapter for some additional suggestions on skyscraper activities.

# Day Five: The Importance of Communication

## Preparation Required and Materials Needed

Divide the class into two balanced groups based on estimates of problem solving ability and social/communication skills. You will need two each of the following size pieces of quarter inch plywood, maisonette, or similar material: 12" by 18", 12" by 24", 12" by 26", 12" by 28". You will also need Beware of Gators (see end of chapter), Avoid Floating Body Parts signs (see end of chapter), and masking tape. Prepare an alley about 20' long. Mark the start and finish line on the floor with the masking tape and decorate with your signs.

## Lesson Directions

Explain to the groups that the alley is really a river. The river is located in a remote wilderness area and it is teeming with man-eating alligators. To make matters worse, a company of enemy soldiers is chasing the group. The soldiers are skilled fighters and heavily armed, they will surely kill the entire group if they catch them. The only weakness the soldiers have is that they cannot swim. The group's challenge is to use teamwork and problem solving to get everyone across the river to safety. You may run one group at a time or two groups simultaneously. If you choose to run two groups simultaneously, you will need to construct two alleys. A stopwatch to add the element of time can be fun. Explain the following conditions and rules to your students, and let them solve the problem.

- Each group has four boards (one of each length).
- The boards can be used to make a floating bridge. Because the river has a current, someone must always be in contact with the boards. An unattended board drifts away (actually, it is kicked away by the teacher).
- All group members must get across.
- All boards must be carried across. If not, the soldiers will use them to get across. Bring the boards with you and you are safe; the soldiers cannot swim.

- A body part that accidentally touches the water may be lost to a hungry gator (teacher discretion).

Process the activity with your students: Did everyone feel supported/included? Did any roles emerge? Did anyone accept a leader's role? Was there only one leader? How did the group solve the challenge? Were there times when you thought you would not get across? If so, what did you do? Was it fun? Did we learn anything that might help us solve our classroom problems? Do you want to try again with one less board?

If you had too much fun to stop, simply issue a new challenge and try again. This time, the groups took a drink from the river, not knowing that the water was infected. All members contracted a virus that left them deaf (no-verbal communication).

Process with your students: Was it harder this time? How important is verbal communication to group problem solving? This time, we had too little verbal communication, but what happens when you have too much (i.e., everyone talks at once)?

Chapter III *The Foundation: Getting to Know Each Other* **27**

# This Is Me

3 things I'm proud of
_____
_____
_____

Why did you choose =>=>=>
_____
_____
_____
_____

What do you like about =>=>
_____
_____
_____
___

3 things I like to do.
_____
_____
_____

Animal that I identify with

[ drawing box ]

Do your best drawing.

3 words ending in "ing" that describe me.
_____
_____
_____

<=<=<=Other Information
_____
_____
_____

3 people I respect/admire/love
_____
_____
_____

Name: _____ Date _____

# This is Me

Alternate Information

Consider having your students list:

- Things they are good at, not good at
- Things they are not proud of
- Things they like to eat
- Places they like to go
- Games they like to play
- Movie favorites
- Favorite songs
- Favorite musical groups
- Favorite baseball, basketball, sports teams
- Favorite cartoons
- Favorite TV shows
- Favorite holidays
- People they would love to meet
- People who make them angry
- Heroes

# States/Abbreviations Matching List

| | | | | | |
|---|---|---|---|---|---|
| Alabama | AL | Massachusetts | MA | South Carolina | SC |
| Alaska | AK | Michigan | MI | South Dakota | SD |
| Arizona | AZ | Minnesota | MN | Tennessee | TN |
| Arkansas | AR | Mississippi | MS | Texas | TX |
| California | CA | Missouri | MO | Utah | UT |
| Colorado | CO | Montana | MT | Vermont | VT |
| Connecticut | CT | Nebraska | NE | Virginia | VA |
| Delaware | DE | Nevada | NV | Virgin Islands | VI |
| Florida | FL | New Hampshire | NH | Washington | WA |
| Georgia | GA | New Jersey | NJ | West Virginia | WV |
| Hawaii | HI | New Mexico | NM | Wisconsin | WI |
| Idaho | ID | New York | NY | Wyoming | WY |
| Illinois | IL | North Carolina | NC | | |
| Indiana | IN | North Dakota | ND | | |
| Iowa | IA | Ohio | OH | | |
| Kansas | KS | Oklahoma | OK | | |
| Kentucky | KY | Oregon | OR | | |
| Louisiana | LA | Pennsylvania | PA | | |
| Maine | ME | Rhode Island | RI | | |
| Maryland | MD | | | | |

# Avoid Floating Body Parts

Chapter III *The Foundation: Getting to Know Each Other* **31**

# Beware of Gators

# Extending Activities

## Community Conversation Boards

Post a large (for a class of twenty-five, about a 30" by 48") piece of roll paper or newsprint with a single teacher generated prompt on it and ask that upon entering the classroom students finish the prompt with their own ideas. Use the Community Conversation Boards as a starting place for class discussions or Classroom Community Meetings. Place your boards in the same place, include a marker on a string, and your kids will soon know what to do when a new board appears. Some prompts are:

- A Classroom Community has...
- Community means...
- A good way to respond to teasing is...
- I get angry when...
- When I am upset I...
- A great field trip would be...
- Other...

## Community Circle of Names and More

Form a circle and hand a soft type of ball or beanbag around the circle, hand to hand. Before you hand the ball to the next person, you say your name and something you like that begins with the first letter of your name, i.e. "John - Jokes." When the ball makes it all around the circle and returns to you, call out someone else's name, i.e. "Bob" and if possible, your memory of the thing Bob associated with his name, i.e. "Bob - Basketball." Then gently toss the ball (underhand) to Bob. Bob does the same thing and gently tosses it to someone else. Continue for a while, and if you want to make things more interesting, add a second or third ball. Processing questions include:

- Was this easy or hard?
- Was it a fun way to learn each other names?
- Is eye contact important?
- Is tossing underhanded important?

## Community Commons

The idea of this activity is to provide your students with a visual/physical representation of the many things community members have in common, while also demonstrating that it's O.K. to differ. Finally, this activity can help your students consider the idea that they may have different things in common with different people. My experience has been that children/young people tend to view people as either just like themselves or totally different. Individuals who hold this perception tend to limit the people they will seek out as potential friends. It is best to do this activity in an open area, i.e. gymnasium, playground, etc. Simply ask your students to form and re-form groups based on the directives you will give them. Tell them to take a look around at who is standing with them after each move. Some standard directives include:

- All people who are wearing tops with a collar, without a collar.
- Everyone wearing blue jeans, black jeans, any other color jeans, anything but jeans.
- Everyone whose favorite fast food is McDonalds, Burger King, Wendy's, Taco Bell.
- Everyone who likes cheese pizza, sausage pizza, veggie pizza, any other kind of pizza.
- Everyone whose favorite sport is football, baseball, basketball, hockey, other.
- Everyone whose favorite music is rock and roll, rap, heavy metal, alternative, country, other.
- Everyone who likes school, hates school, is in the middle.
- All people who are the only child, have brothers, have sisters, have both.
- Everyone who thinks the most important quality for a good friend is honesty, popularity, loyalty, physical strength, physical appearance.
- All people who would choose their job based on how much money you can make, where the job is located, the type and quality of the work, the people you would work with.

Obviously, this can be a lighthearted or very serious activity. Naturally I encourage you to write directives to fit your community and your issues. Process with your students: Were you surprised how much you had in common? Were you surprised how much you differed? Were you ever surprised at who was in your group? Did groups tend to stay the same or change? Was there anyone who went to all the same groups as you? Were there any lessons for daily life in our Classroom Community? Was it fun?

## Skyscraper Fun

Ask your students to bring in things from home to decorate their skyscraper. You can supply yarn, ribbon, ornaments, student artwork, academic work, etc. This can be a planned activity, but I have had more fun just introducing the idea and letting the kids decorate as individuals as the urge hits them. Let this happen over a two-week period and you may have a work of modern art.

# Chapter IV

# THE CLASSROOM COMMUNITY MODEL

> *The circle is a sacred symbol of life . . .*
> *Individual parts within the circle connect*
> *With every other; and what happens to*
> *one, or what one part does affects all*
> *within the circle.*
> -Virginia Driving Hawk Sneve-

## Outcomes

1. Students will be able to define "Community."
2. Students will be able to define "Classroom Community."
3. Students will be able to list key elements of a Classroom Community.
4. Students will decide on specific activities, procedures, and items they believe will transform their classroom into a Classroom Community.

## Teacher Information

You have already spent some time helping your students get to know each other, relax with each other, and trust each other. You have set in place a foundation upon which to build a Classroom Community. Today's lesson marks the start of the formal building process. Remember that we have defined a Classroom Community as a social organization, one whose reason to exist is to provide educational opportunities to its members. Remember too that we enumerated learner outcomes that went beyond reading, writing, and arithmetic. We included learner outcomes in the areas of personal and social responsibility. In order to help your students become responsible citizens, you must be willing to give them responsibility. The journey to responsibility starts here. Even young children possess ample experiences with communities to allow them to participate easily in this introductory lesson. If you experience some difficulty getting them started, it is probably because they do not associate the term community with the many communities with which they are familiar. Once the definition of the word community is shared and an example or two provided, the lesson always flows smoothly. Approximate instructional time for this component is three (3) class periods.

# Day One: Defying Gravity

## Preparation Required and Materials Needed

A chalkboard and room enough to form circles of eight to ten students.

## Lesson Directions

Discuss some of your foundation/get-to-know-and-trust-each-other activities. Ask if your students trust you. Ask for a volunteer and suggest that the volunteer should be someone who feels very confident about doing physical things. Ask the class and the volunteer if they know what the effects of gravity are. Ask the volunteer how far someone can lean backwards from a standing position (without bending at the waist or knees) before gravity would win and that person would lose balance. Ask your volunteer to illustrate the point where that person would lose balance by drawing a dotted line between the two solid perpendicular lines you have already drawn on the board. Most students will grossly over-estimate the ability to maintain balance. This only adds to the lesson's fun.

## Illustration

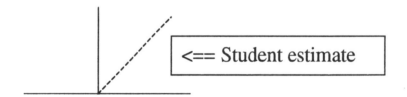

Tell the student that you only know one way to see if that estimate is accurate. Tell the volunteer that you will position yourself behind him or her and that you will be there when he or she loses balance. Ask the volunteer to lean backward until he or she loses balance. You can now place a solid line on the chalkboard indicating the point the student's balance was actually lost. Some kids will want to dispute your evaluation, again presenting a wonderful opportunity for friendly bantering and relationship development. You can resume the original position, ask the student to once again learn backwards, and this time, stop at the point balance is lost and hold the student there. If there is still a doubt, remove your support and find out who is correct. At this point, you should have the whole class actively engaged and cheering the friendly interaction on. Thank your volunteer and ask him or her to be seated. Tell the class that as a group, a community, you think they could do a better job of defying gravity. Tell them that no matter how physically fit or how great an athlete, no individual could do any better than your volunteer. Tell them that even if you gave them all a month to work out for the gravity test, they could not significantly improve their individual performances.

Tell the class that if they will work together, support each other, and trust each other you think you have a way to help every individual in the room defy gravity, but only as part of a group of individuals working together. Divide the class into groups of ten to twelve students. Have the groups form circles with everyone facing in toward the center of the circle. Now direct every other individual to turn around so that they face out or away from the circle's, center. Ask the groups to join hands. Grips must be firm as they must support the weight of the people they are holding on to. The circle should be large enough to cause each member to feel some tension from people to their immediate left and right. Have your students count off by 2's (1,2, . . . 1,2 . . . 1, 2). Tell them that on your direction the 1's will lean in and the 2's will lean out. Tell them this will only work if they lean slowly and deliberately, if they move in unison, if they all commit to the lean and hold the commitment. Tell the kids that if they really start to lose their balance, all they need to do is step forward with either foot. Tell them to start their lean on your count of three (1-2-3). Switch the direction of 1's and 2's and try it again. Switch the direction individuals face and try again. Celebrate your success or at least your honest attempt. Tell the kids that you will give them time over the next two weeks to practice their "Community Circle of Support." Explain that you believe that, working together, you think they will be able to go on their own count and to reverse the in and out motion without having to come to a complete stop, sort of a wave motion. Tell them you want them to experiment on their own and see what they can do. Have everyone return to their seats. Watch the progress over the next two weeks. Step in only if there are safety issues (physical or psychological).

Process the Activity: How did you feel working together? Did you feel safe, supported, included? How did the direction you faced affect your experience? Did it feel good to improve your performance? Did it feel good to support each other? How can we support each other in class? Do you think you will be able to get the wave? Was it fun?

End by asking your students to give some thought to what a "community" is, and to communities they belong to. One option is to have your students interview their parents to get their parents' definition of a "community" as a homework assignment.

## Day Two Defining Community

## Preparation Required and Materials Needed

Write out or think through a definition of community and a definition of a Classroom Community. Think through or compile a list of example communities. You will find sample definitions and lists of communities and teacher lecture notes at the end of the chapter. You will need newsprint or roll paper, a marker, and some masking tape.

## Lesson Directions

Ask your students for their definition of Community. If you chose to assign the parent interview for homework, students may share their parents' responses. Ask for characteristics and components of a community. Ask why they think people choose to live in communities and what they think the benefits are. The teacher or a student should serve as a recorder, putting the classes' ideas on the newsprint for future reference. Ask for examples of communities to which your students belong and list these on a separate piece of newsprint. Draft a generic definition of a community. Ask if they think your classroom could be a community. Explain the Classroom Community Model (see end of chapter lecture notes). Have the class write their Classroom Community definition and record it on newsprint. Display newsprint products for all to see. It is important that students see artifacts of the process and the effort you used to arrive at your Classroom Community definition. After a few days, you may want to dispose of everything but the actual Classroom Community definition; this should continue to be displayed. Your definition should be just that: your definition. Some sample definitions, however, have been included for your convenience at the end of the chapter.

## Day Three: Things That Make a Community

### Preparation Required and Materials Needed

"A Classroom Community Has" Worksheet and the worksheet's sample answers. You will also need newsprint or roll paper and a marker.

### Lesson Directions

Have your class divide into groups no larger than six students. You may wish to divide into diads or triads. In any case, the assignment is for the groups to complete the "A Classroom Community Has" Worksheet and report out the work groups' answers to a recorder who records answers on newsprint, forming a composite list. If you feel your students are mature enough, you may instruct them to only offer answers that have not been previously offered. While this procedure is efficient, younger, less mature students can feel cheated. If you choose to use this procedure simply instruct groups to line out answers as they are given by other groups. You may want to have the recorder simply place tally marks by answers that are repeated. This provides an indication of the popularity of individual answers.

Evaluate your composite list and eliminate any you are not comfortable with. Always give your students the courtesy of sharing your thinking. It is a good idea to implement as many ideas as soon as possible. You are being watched to see if you really mean all that stuff about giving the students more power (responsibility) and about building a community.

# Community Definitions

Community: *A group of people living in the same place and under the same laws.*

Community: *A group of people living in the same place who share similar values and customs. As a community, these people live under laws that support their values.*

Classroom
Community: *A group of students who believe that, by working together, they will be able to achieve great things. A group of students who accept and live by the same rules, respect each other as individuals, help each other to reach personal goals, do their part to attain community goals, and watch out for and care for one another.*

Classroom
Community: *A group of students who want to be kind and respectful to each other, who want to learn a lot and have a lot of fun.*

# Teacher Lecture Notes: Classroom Community Model

A Classroom Community Is A Class Where:

- Students are given opportunities to get to know each other (refer to some of your foundation Activities)

- Students build helping relationships

- Students learn about making decisions and solving problems

- Students work together in weekly community meetings to help run their classroom and to solve community issues and individual community members' problems.

- Students are given a lot of help to solve problems and work out solutions in the community before anyone else is involved, i.e. dean, principal, parents.

- Students are given a lot of responsibility for how things are done and wherever possible asked to participate in decisions regarding everyday classroom life.

- Everyone works together to learn as much as possible while having as much fun as is possible.

- Suggest that they begin thinking of the class as community. Tell them that like it or not once the principal made the class list they were destined to spend about 180 days or 1080 hours together.

- Ask if they would rather spend it in a community?

# Example Communities

- Family

- Church

- School

- Clubs

- Teams

- Town/Cities

- States

- Gangs

# A Classroom Community Has

Date Completed_____

List your class' definition of a Classroom Community and refer to it as you make your suggestions_____
_____
_____
_____
_____
_____
_____
_____
_____
_____

## Our Community Has

| | |
|---|---|
| _____ | _____ |
| _____ | _____ |
| _____ | _____ |
| _____ | _____ |
| _____ | _____ |
| _____ | _____ |
| _____ | _____ |
| _____ | _____ |
| _____ | _____ |

Team Member's Initials

_____  _____  _____
_____  _____  _____
_____  _____  _____

# A Classroom Community Has: Possible Answers

NOTE: This list is a composite of answers provided by many student and teacher work groups.

- Decorate the room - plants, posters, soft furniture
- Community bulletin board - photos (baby, family, pets), sayings, quotes, etc.
- Classroom pets
- Classroom jobs
- Celebrations, (birthdays, holidays)
- Take turns bringing in snacks
- Choose free time activities
- Choose reinforcements
- Learning partners, Cooperative learning
- Music
- Choose some of our assignments
- Homework passes
- Games
- Get to move around
- Group art project (mural)
- Group T-shirts, Group Nickname
- Give each other back rubs when we need them
- Sharing something from home we like
- Make our own seating arrangements
- A quiet area we can choose to go to
- Write our own room song
- Board games
- Have talent show
- Do plays
- Choose some field trips
- Pick what we talk about at classroom meetings
- Homework buddies
- Get to interview a classmate and introduce them to the community
- Get to make videos
- Make special name tags
- Run a classroom business to make money for classroom activities
- Get to work in study groups
- Get to tutor younger students
- Get extra help for my students who need it (senior citizen tutors)
- Get involved in a community service project

# Extending Activities

## Working Together To Defy Gravity

Have students work in groups of eight. Give each group either a six foot length of sturdy wood closet rod or a ten foot length of rope (both props must be strong enough to support the heaviest students' weight). Ask your students to use their props to help one member defy gravity. The challenge is to get one group member's face as close to the floor as possible without any other portion of that group member's body touching the floor except their feet. The person's body must be rigid (no bending at the knees, waist, or neck). No one may actually touch the person except for the group member securing the person's feet. Safety rules:

1. feet stay on the ground
2. face always faces ground
3. spotter secures feet
4. spotter protects head
5. rope or rod is never higher than the armpits

Ask your students the following questions.

- How did you decide what to do?
- How did you decide who would defy gravity?
- What roles did you assume?
- Did the individual feel safe, supported?
- Did the individual like the attention?
- Can you think of a time when it helps if everyone chips in to help an Individual?
- Do you think we will have the opportunity to do so in our Classroom Community?
- Was it fun?

## Community Essay

Have students write essays that

- Describe their Classroom Community
- Compare/Contrast a Classroom Community to a traditional classroom
- Describe what an individual community member can do to support the community

## Community Poem/Song

Have students write poems/songs illustrating what it means to be part of a Classroom Community.

## Art Projects

Have students illustrate your Classroom Community visually. Consider:

- drawings
- paintings
- clay sculptures
- photos
- videos
- collages

## Discussions

Facilitate a Discussion Based on One of the Following Quotes:

*He drew a circle to keep me out.*
*Heretic, rebel a thing to flout.*
*But love and I had the wit to win.*
*We drew a circle that took him in.*
            -Edwin Markham-
            From "Outwitted"

*The circle is a sacred symbol of life . . .*
*Individual parts within the circle connect*
*with every other; and what happens to*
*one, or what one part does affect all*
*within the circle.*
            Virginia Driving Hawk Sneve

*Teambuilding Is for the Birds; Not Such a Silly goose.*
            -Source Unknown

## Team Building is for the Birds

## Not Such A Silly Goose

*Next fall, when you see geese heading south for the winter,.flying along in a V formation,..you may consider what science has discovered as to why they fly that way.*

*As each bird flaps its wings, it creates an uplift for the bird immediately following. By flying V formation the whole flock adds at least 71 percent greater flying range than if each bird flew on its own.*

*People who share a common direction and sense of community can get where they're going more quickly and easily because they are traveling on the thrust of one another.*

*When a goose falls out of formation it suddenly feels the drag and resistance of trying to go it alone..and quickly gets back into formation to take advantage of the lifting power of the bird in front.*

*If we have as much sense as a goose, we will stay in formation with those who are headed the same way we are. When the head goose gets tired it rotates back in the wing, and another goose files in point.*
*It is sensible to take turns doing demanding jobs with people or with geese flying south. Geese honk from behind to encourage those up front to keep up the speed. What do we say when we honk from behind?*

*Finally,.and this is important..when a goose gets sick, or is wounded by gunshots and falls out of formation, two other geese fall out with the goose and follow it down to lend help and protection. They stay with the fallen goose until it is able to fly or until it dies; and only then do they launch out on their own, or with another formation to catch up with their group.*

*If we have the sense of a goose we will stand by each other like that.*

-Source unknown

# Chapter V

# CONTRACTS

> *Rules without relationships equal rebellion.*

## Outcomes

1. Students will identify shared values for their Classroom Community Contracts.
2. Students will write rules to support their shared values.
3. Students will develop a range of positive and negative outcomes.
4. Students will take part in a meaningful democratic decision making process.

## Teacher Information

*Rules without relationship equals rebellion.* The first time I heard these words, they were part of a talk given by a minister. The minister wanted parents to understand that more important than any rule they might establish for their children was the relationship they had the opportunity to build and nurture with them. He also used the same words in another way. He said that children were more likely to obey a rule if they understood the relationship between the rule and the value it supported. While I certainly do not have the minister's way with words, I know I have been telling teachers for years that everything they do or fail to do in their classrooms is based on the relationships they have with their students and the relationships their students have with each other. I have also spent a lot of time convincing teachers that kids support rules that support sound values. I have been asking teachers to extend to their students the same consideration and respect we as adults demand. How many of you appreciate knowing the rationale behind the latest rule to govern teacher behavior? How many of you demand to know? We are people, not sheep, and we need to know the reason "why" anytime our individual freedom is curtailed.

School Boards and administrators always talk about making sure the teachers buy in on the ground floor. They know that for any new initiative to succeed, their teachers must understand the need to change. They need to see the ultimate benefit. It is the same with your students. Having your students write Classroom Community Contracts gives your students a new, refreshing, and empowering message. It tells them that their teacher:

1. Respects their opinion and ultimately believes in them.
2. Believes that they are serious about their education and their Classroom Community.
3. Expects them to take responsibility for their individual behavior and the

general climate of their Classroom Community.
4. Understands the importance of buying in on the ground floor and is giving them the opportunity to do so.

# Classroom Community Contracts

Contracts are agreements made between the members of a Classroom Community about what the community values, about the basic rights and responsibilities of individuals, about the rules required to support the values and rights established, and about outcomes for classroom behavior.

It is recommended that you write four to six contracts. Classroom Community Contracts are made up of three primary components: Values, Rules, and Outcomes. Values are defined as principles or ideals the community shares, and rules are defined as behavioral manifestations of those values, or the usual or agreed upon way of doing something. Outcomes are defined as the effects of behavior. The effect or results of behavior may be positive or negative.

# Meaningful Values

Meaningful values are values that give direction to Classroom Community behavior. A good value points to specific rules and behaviors. It gives purpose to and justification for the rules that support it. Ultimately, it is an expression of the community's value system and is indicative of what the community holds to be most important. Values are extremely important, and general in nature and language. Values are not written to be measured or enforced. Instead, they make a general statement about what individual rights and responsibilities will look like in a particular classroom community.

# Examples of meaningful values are:

- Courtesy
- Physical safety
- Psychological safety
- Knowledge
- Respect
- Freedom to have an opinion
- Dignity, privacy, and personal space

Chapter V *Contracts* **49**

# Practical Rules

Practical rules are rules that operationalize values. They are behavioral manifestations of the values. Rules define which behaviors are acceptable and which are not. Effective rules are directly related to the value they support. If a rule is a good rule, this relationship requires little or no explanation. Rules should be specific, but how specific is a function of the age of the students, their understanding of language, and their individual and social maturity. A rule must be specific enough to delineate behavioral expectations; it does not have to mention every possible infraction. In fact, this "shopping list" method leads to confusion, as in reality, it is impossible to list every infraction. This method sets the teacher and student up for arguments. The preferred method is to spend time discussing rules until you are sure your students have a clear understanding of what a particular rule means. It is recommended that you write no more than six specific rules per contract. Stress that the importance of the specific rules is their ability to support a community value. Explain to your students that you will use common sense when helping them determine if they broke a rule, but that, more importantly, you will help them determine if their behavior supported or undermined a community value. When writing rules, attempt to be concise and to the point. Be clear and be brief. When at all possible, [...] rule in positive terms. For example, "keep hands and feet to yourself" [...] kick." This will not always be possible. In this case, write the rule

[...]ctical rules are:

[...]nds and feet to yourself.
[...]e speaker to finish before you begin speaking.
[...] to solve your own problem, answer your own question, and ask
[...]ning partner before raising your hand.
[...]r hand to be called on.
[...]larification before assuming intent.
[...]e using someone's things.

[...]tive Outcomes

[...]f the outcome to the rule and behavior should be clear and easily [...]dent. This is necessary for the development of individual [...]tely an internal locus of control. In the case of a rule/behavior infraction, the outcome will, of course, be negative. Negative outcomes should be as natural as possible. For example, if you go out in the cold without a coat and hat, you will get sick. Establishing this relationship, although optimal, is not always possible. When natural is not possible, opt for logical; i.e., if you fail to do your arithmetic during class, you will finish it during your free period. Negative outcomes must be reasonable. They should not go overboard; i.e., you wrote on your desk, so you will wash all twenty-eight desks in the room. Care should always be taken that negative outcomes respect the student as a person, and that the student's dignity is preserved. There is a difference between "we can discuss this here (in class)" and "let's talk privately in the hall." Finally, the Classroom Community contract, or any other convention, must not supersede the teacher's judgment in determining the nature and degree of a negative outcome. A good contract includes outcomes that offer the teacher a range of alternatives.

## Examples of Positive Outcomes

- Pay attention, do in-class assignments, and homework assignments, - I will do well on tests.

- Ask for help only after I have attempted to answer my own question, solve my own problem, ask my learning partner — I become an independent learner and my teacher is available for those who really need her (including me).

- Keep hands and feet to self— everyone feels and is safe.

## Examples of Negative Outcomes:

- Fail to pay attention, do class work, homework assignments, — I do poorly on tests.

- Ask for help as soon as I think I might not be able to answer my own question or solve my own problem - I stay a dependent learner, my teacher is seldom available for those who really need help (including me).

- Fail to keep hands and feet to self, hit classmates — I lose friends, people avoid me, I may be suspended, I make my community an unsafe place to be.

Classroom Community contracts become a guide for all subsequent classroom behavior. They serve as a benchmark against which to measure behavior. When writing Classroom Community contracts, the teacher will do well to keep the adage "the process is more important than the product" in mind. The process allows and, if done correctly, encourages students to buy into the concept of a Classroom Community. It asks them to create an environment where they can be successful. It provides them the opportunity to engage in an open discussion with their teacher and their classmates about the upcoming year, its possibilities, and its potential pitfalls. It fosters responsible relationships. It continues to expose the students to the concepts of individual and social responsibility. It builds on the theme of community. Most importantly, it establishes the need for any community, including an educational community, to have a purpose or a reason to form and to continue to exist. It helps students to begin to see that for any community to be successful and for individuals within the community to work in concert, rules become a necessity. It ultimately must make clear the relationship between the basic community values and the rules and behavioral outcomes written to support them. While many students will obey rules without questioning them, an increasing number of students will not. For these students, the process of writing Classroom Community contracts sets the stage for rule compliance. This is not blind compliance, but thoughtful, informed, involved compliance. This type of compliance builds individual and social responsibility. The importance of involving students in some type of democratic process whereby they play a primary role in determining the classroom climate can not be overstated. The work of Curwin and Mendler (1988), Gathercoal (1991), Hill (1985), and Jones and Jones (1990) support it.

## When writing Classroom Community Contracts, make sure to:

- Provide a forum that encourages open and honest discussion. This means input from all factions of the class, i.e., the good students, the goof-offs, the jocks and rah/rahs, the gifted, and the slow learners. Student involvement is everything.

- Discuss the reason you (the teacher) decided to ask the class to write the Classroom Community Contracts instead of writing them yourself and just sharing them with the class. Explain to your students that people work better and harder, are more successful, and enjoy themselves more when they are involved in setting their own working and living conditions.

- Use the time you spend writing Classroom Community Contracts to build relationships with and among your students. Your ability to facilitate your students living by the Classroom Community Contracts they write will largely be dependent upon the quality of the relationship you have with them. Your students' willingness to support a classmate struggling to meet the standards of your Classroom Community Contracts will be enhanced if healthful relationships have already been established among the students.

- Are there values or rules that are a must for you (the teacher)? If so, let your students know and present these as your nonnegotiable values/rules. I strongly suggest keeping these to a minimum.

- Develop contracts that are "consistently inconsistent." By consistent, I mean that what is right will always be right and what is wrong will always be wrong. This way, productive, responsible behavior is easily distinguishable from non-productive, irresponsible behavior (rule violations). What is inconsistent is how the teacher and, in some instances, the community, responds to the rule violation. Outcomes must provide the teacher a series (not hierarchy) of alternative consequences from which to choose. The teacher has the opportunity to match the outcome not only to specific behavior but also to particular circumstances. These circumstances include the purpose of the behavior, the emotional stability and social maturity of the student(s) involved, and any other factor the teacher believes should be included in the determination of the outcomes. Remind your students that "fair" in your community does not always mean equal. Also remind them that one person's right will always be the other person's responsibility.

- Discuss logical outcomes and make sure that these are included in the Classroom Community Contracts. Help your students to be reasonable when writing outcomes. If they are like most groups I have worked with, they will be overly punitive and harsh.

- Let your students know that you will regularly review your Classroom Community Contracts and make changes as it becomes logical to do so. This will help your students to relax and participate freely, not worrying that they may make a mistake that will haunt them the entire year. You also communicate your understanding that the class' needs and concerns may change, and that you are interested in changing with them.

- Are you secure enough to ask your students to develop rules for you? If so, ask them to write no more than one rule specifically addressing teacher behavior for each value. Note: Sample contracts and a contract form are included at the end of the chapter.

## Day One Through Six: Writing Contracts

### Preparation Required and Materials Needed

If you choose the option of having students work in small groups to write rules and outcomes, newsprint or roll paper and markers (enough for each group) are required.

### Lesson Directions

The procedure for actually writing your Classroom Community Contracts is simple. Role playing can be an effective tool for evaluating rules and outcomes. It does slow things down, but remember, the process is more important than the product. Follow these basic steps:

- Introduce the concept of Classroom Community Contracts. Discuss how they fit within the larger context of the Classroom Community. Explain the process you will use to develop your Classroom Community Contracts. Share some Contract examples. Explain what makes a sound value sound, go over the basic elements of an effective rule, and discuss positive and negative outcomes.

- Convene a teacher led community discussion to select four to six values. Selection of values can usually be accomplished in one to two class periods. It is strongly recommended that you select and discuss all of your Community values prior to writing rules and developing outcomes. Convene a series of community discussions to write rules and outcomes for each value. Do one value at a time, writing both the rules and outcomes for that value. It usually takes one period per value. Reduce your Classroom Community Contracts to writing. Use the Contract Form included in this book or be creative. Your contracts should be displayed for all community members to see.

## Teacher Implementation Options

- You might want to assign homework as part of the contract writing process. Suggestions include having students write a value, a rule, or an outcome to bring to a classroom discussion. If you do so, it can be helpful to collect the homework in time to pull duplicates prior to the meeting. This job can be assigned to a student volunteer; this supports the notion that individual students are responsible for their Classroom Community.

- Good results have been achieved by using Cooperative Learning strategies or just having students work in triads or small groups to prepare for the full community discussions. In this way, you promote student-to-student relationships, group skills, and set the stage for very productive community meetings. Most often, teachers will have work groups write rules and/or outcomes to present to the Full Community. Work groups can record their answers on newsprint for Community Sharing.

- Many teachers like to use the Constitution as a model for introducing contracts. They explain that, while the Bill of Rights gives citizens certain rights (similar to our value statements), we need laws (similar to our rules) to support the rights. We also have consequences for breaking laws such as fines, tickets, and jail (similar to our negative outcomes).

# Extending Activities

## Visual Representation

Art projects to illustrate your contracts are great as individual or small group activities.

## Video Presentations

Video commercials advertising a community value(s) can really be a great learning experience for all involved. If several classrooms are writing contracts, having each community produce a commercial for their values to be shown at a multi-community or school wide screening is great fun.

## Role Play

Role plays/skits represent a creative way to begin discussing what living by your community contracts might look like.

## Find a Community Member

Complete and process the Find a Community Member Who worksheet. Have students circulate the room attempting to secure a different signature for each task. Process the results with the whole class.

## Community Circle

Complete and process the Community Circle of Caring.

# Finding a Community Member Who . .

**Task: Find someone who --------and get their signature**

1. Has written or signed a contract outside of school

    Signature_____

2. Has family meetings or talks to plan things or solve problems

    Signature_____

3. Never ever breaks school rules

    Signature_____

4. Has a value that they know they will always support

    Signature_____

5. Has a rule that will be especially hard for them to keep

    Signature_____

*Move around the room, attempting to get a different signature for each task.*

# Community Circle of Caring

Complete the numbered pie sections by drawing a symbol, picture, or design to answer the following questions:

1. What can the community do for you to help you feel comfortable?

2. What can you do for the community to help other people feel comfortable?

3. What is the difference between a classroom and a classroom community?

4. What is one goal you have for yourself this year?

5. What is the community's most important value?

6. What is the community's most needed rule?

# Community Circle of Caring

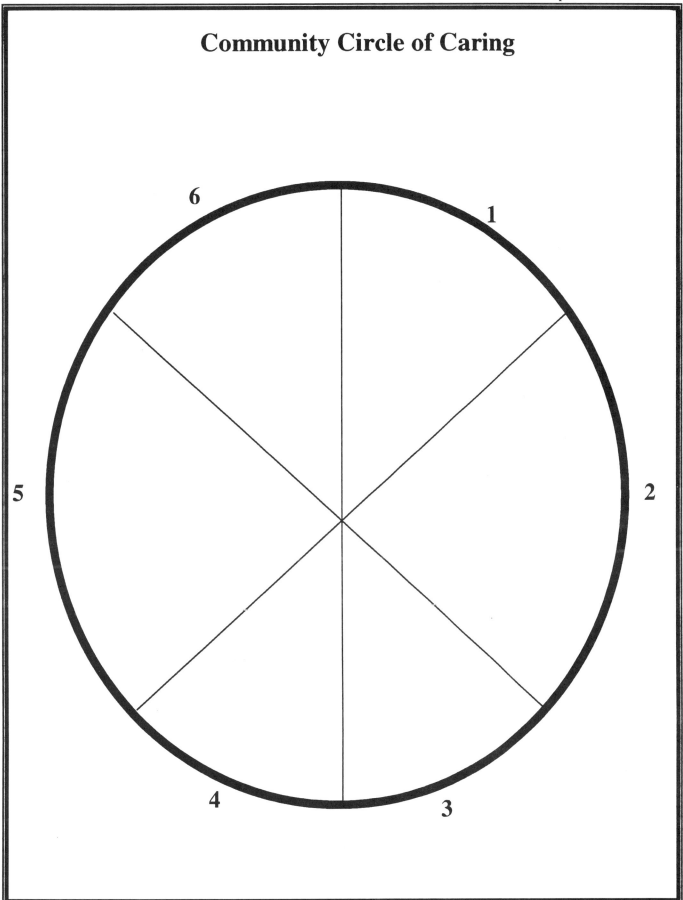

# Classroom Community Contract

Community:_____ Date:_____

Classroom Community Value
_____
_____
_____
_____
_____

Rules
_____
_____
_____
_____
_____
_____
_____
_____

Positive Outcomes:                    Negative Outcomes:
_____             _____
_____             _____
_____             _____
_____             _____
_____             _____
_____             _____
_____             _____
_____             _____

# Sample
# Classroom Community Contract

Community: _____  Date: _____

## Classroom Community Value

*All members of our community have a right to learn.*

_____

## Rules

*Be prepared for class (book, materials, assignments, homework).*

*Attempt to answer my own question, solve my own problem, ask my learning partner if appropriate.*

*Raise hand to get teacher's attention. Wait to be called on.*

| Positive Outcomes: | Negative Outcomes: |
|---|---|
| Being an independent learner. | We always need help |
| Making friends/helpers | Don't get a chance to be helpers |
| Teacher is available | Teacher is seldom free to help |
| Learn more, earn better grades | Learn less, grades suffer |
| Earn weekly free time | Don't earn free time |
| Earn Stand-up slips | Don't earn awards |
| Earn classroom survival awards | Spend time in time out |

# Sample
# Classroom Community Contract

Community:_____ Date:_____

### Classroom Community Value

*We all have the right to be safe.*

### Rules

*In our community we will use "I" messages.*

*In our community, we will keep our hand and feet to ourselves.*

*In our community, we will respect personal space.*

*In our community, there will be no gang representation.*

| Positive Outcomes: | Negative Outcomes: |
|---|---|
| *We will all get along* | *We don't get along* |
| *We talk with each other* | *We fight* |
| *We solve our problems* | *We have unresolved issues* |
| *No one gets hurt* | *People get hurt* |
| *Stand-up slips* | *Supervised lunch* |
| *Student of the week* | *Detention* |
| *Parties* | *Suspension* |

# Sample
# Classroom Community Contract

Community:_____ Date:_____

## Classroom Community Value

*Everyone has the right to be respected and learn.*

## Rules

*Listen to others.*

*Use people's names.*

*Respond to others with positive comments (find solutions instead of blame.*

*Be prepared for class.*

*Complete assignments.*

*Participate in group discussions and class assignments.*

| Positive Outcomes: | Negative Outcomes: |
|---|---|
| *Can do things together* | *No one will listen to you when you talk* |
| *Feel liked* | *People will feel bad* |
| *People will say nice things to you* | *People will say things that hurt you back* |
| *Learner more* | *No one will like you* |
| *Make friends* | *Parent conferences* |
| | *Have to apologize* |
| | *Detentions/external sespensions* |

# Sample
# Classroom Community Contract

Community: _____   Date: _____

Classroom Community Value:

_Everyone has the right to be safe_

**Rules**

_We keep our hands to ourselves_

_We call each other by our names (no cadding)_

_We listen and consider all opinions (no discounting)_

_We give each other the benefit of the doubt and check it out (no he say--she say)._

| Positive Outcomes: | Negative Outcomes: |
|---|---|
| No one will get hurt. | Someone will get hurt. |
| Everyone will trust each other (relax). | People will feel bad. |
| Get to do more in class. | You lose the group's trust. |
| | You lose the group's respect. |
| | Supervised lunch. |
| | Detention. |
| | Time out. |
| | External suspension. |
| | No field trips. |

# Sample
# Classroom Community Contract

Community:_____ Date:_____

## Classroom Community Value

*All members of our community have a right to be themselves.*

_____

## Rules

*Speak our mind using "I" statements.*

*Opinions are OK; we listen to them.*

*Disagree if we want to.*

| Positive Outcomes: | Negative Outcomes: |
|---|---|
| *Earn points.* | *Lose points.* |
| *Our classroom will be more creative.* | *Our classroom will be boring.* |
| *OK to act like yourself.* | *Hurt others' feelings.* |
| *Have more fun in class* | *Feel like we have to act like we are someone else.* |
| *Make different friends* | |

# Sample
# Classroom Community Contract

Community:_____ Date:_____

## Classroom Community Value

*We have the right to speak and be heard.*

## Rules

*Raise you hand when you speak.*

*Really listen to person speaking.*

| Positive Outcomes: | Negative Outcomes: |
|---|---|
| *We learn.* | *We don't learn* |
| *We show and are given respect.* | *We lose respect.* |
| *Everyone has a turn to speak.* | *We might not get a turn.* |
| *Everyone will be heard.* | *Detention* |
| *Stand-up slip* | *Supervised lunch* |
| *Parties.* | *Student of the week* |

Chapter V *Contracts* **65**

# Sample
# Classroom Community Contract

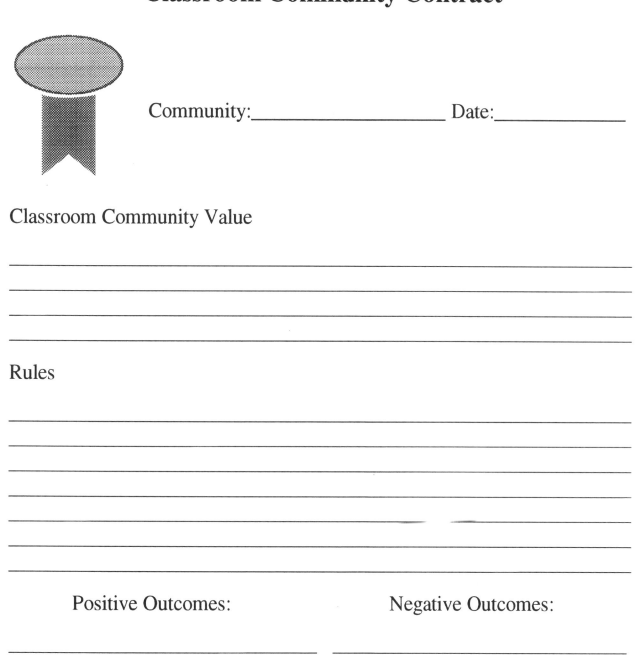

Community:_____ Date:_____

Classroom Community Value

_____
_____
_____
_____

Rules

_____
_____
_____
_____
_____
_____
_____

Positive Outcomes:                    Negative Outcomes:

_____        _____
_____        _____
_____        _____
_____        _____
_____        _____
_____        _____

# Sample
# Classroom Community Contract

Community:_____ Date_____

Classroom Community Value

_____
_____
_____

Rules

_____
_____
_____
_____
_____
_____

Positive Outcomes:                    Negative Outcomes:

_____          _____
_____          _____
_____          _____
_____          _____
_____          _____

# Sample
# Classroom Community Contract

Community:_____ Date:_____

Classroom Community Value

_____
_____
_____
_____

Rules

_____
_____
_____
_____
_____
_____
_____
_____

Positive Outcomes:                    Negative Outcomes:

_____        _____
_____        _____
_____        _____
_____        _____
_____        _____
_____        _____
_____        _____

# Chapter VI
# MOTIVATION AND BASIC NEEDS

*I did it again. I'm in trouble and I have no idea why I did what I did.*

## Outcomes

1. Students will be able to list basic needs. Students will differentiate between physiological and psychological needs.
2. Students will develop an understanding of the relationship between basic needs and behavior.
3. Students will discuss the difference between meeting needs responsibly and irresponsibly.
4. Students will inventory and then expand the ways needs can be met in their Classroom Community.

## Teacher Information

All behavior is purposeful. Everything we do is done to help us to meet a Basic physiological or psychological need (Glasser 1993). As adults, much of our time is spent in behavior that enables us to meet our physiological needs. We go to work to earn money so that we can stop to buy food, cook the food and finally eat the food. In order to meet just one of our physiological needs we engaged in the following behaviors: (1) working; (2) shopping; (3) cooking; (4) eating. All behavior was purposeful, all directed at meeting our need for sustenance. The relationship between behavior and need is clear and easily understood.

The relationship between our psychological needs and the behaviors we engage in to meet these needs is sometimes not quite as clear. It certainly is more difficult to understand, or at least more complex. Yet the relationship between our psychological needs and our behavior is no less real. We all have a basic need to be connected to other human beings, a need to <u>belong</u>. In order to satisfy this need, we have families, we live in communities, we join clubs and organizations, we build and work hard to maintain friendships. We have a need to be <u>competent,</u> so we learn new skills, set and achieve goals, become teachers, carpenters, and doctors. We have a need to be <u>independent,</u> so we choose our hairstyles, our friends, our schools, our careers, and our mates. We even open our own businesses so that we can be our own bosses. We have a need to have <u>fun,</u> so we go to the movies, we tell jokes, we listen to music, we enjoy each other's company, and we work out. Much of what we do or choose not to do is driven by our psychological needs. If we understand the relationship between our needs and our behaviors, we can more effectively direct and control our behaviors. As teachers, we often attempt to figure out the need or desire underlying a child's behavior. We know that if we understand why children are misbehaving, we have a much better chance of helping those children to correct or change their behavior. In a Classroom Community, we empower our students through sharing our knowledge of human behavior with them. We teach our students about needs, behavior, and motivation. We put them in situations such as Classroom Community Meetings and Individual Responsibility Plan Development to use the information to take control of their individual outcomes. We further require them to positively influence the outcomes of their fellow community members and the community as a whole. By providing this information, we continue to position our students to develop the all-important internal locus of control. Instructional time for this component is approximately three (3) class periods.

## Day One: Learning To Plan

### Preparation Required and Materials Needed

Newsprint or roll paper and markers for small group work.

### Lesson Directions

Explain that everyone has the same basic human needs: physiological needs (food, water, shelter, etc.) and psychological needs (belonging, competency, independence, and fun). Tell your students that while we are not always aware of it, all our behavior is purposeful and everything we do or choose not to do is directed at helping us meet one or more of our basic needs. Use the example of meeting your need for food to teach how behavior is related to need gratification. In order to meet your need for food, you engage in the certain behaviors. Work to earn money. Shop to buy food. Cook to prepare the food. Eat to ingest the food. Explain that all four behaviors were purposeful and directed at meeting your need for food. The need for food drove or motivated you to undertake certain behaviors.

Tell your students that the relationship between our psychological needs (belonging, competency, independence, and fun) and the behaviors we engage in to meet these needs is not always as clear. Explain that in school, we primarily engage in behavior directed at meeting psychological needs. Explain that most of their physiological needs are taken care of at home or are already in place when they come to school. For example, we wear a coat to keep warm, we bring a lunch to eat, washroom breaks are scheduled, etc. Note: This can spark a lively discussion as some students may be quick to point out how their physiological needs are not adequately addressed at school, for example, not enough heat, bad or not enough food, not enough washroom breaks, etc. This is good grist for the Classroom Community Meeting mill.

Tell your students that in social systems (Classroom Community, School Community) there are reasonable ways to meet their psychological needs, ways that do not stop other people from meeting their needs. There are ways that do not disrupt the purpose of the community (remind them that in school the community purpose is to learn) and ways that do not endanger them or other people. For example, the need to <u>belong</u> might be met by joining the math club, basketball team, school play, or a gang. The need for <u>competency</u> could be met by studying hard and earning good grades or bullying other students. The need to have <u>fun</u> can be met by having a sense of humor in class or by being a class clown who stops the learning process. The need for <u>independence</u> could be met by choosing a group topic for the Social Studies project, or by choosing not to do a project. The needs are the same; the behaviors are quite different.

Emphasize that needs are human, and that everyone has the right to have their basic human needs met. However, the behavior we engage in to help meet our needs must be adaptive and fair. Explain that adaptive means "has a reasonable chance of success," and that fair means "is safe for all involved and does not limit the rights of others to meet their needs." Tell your students that you would like to give them the opportunity to better define each of the four psychological needs by identifying some of the feelings associated with the needs.

Divide your students into four groups. Assign each group one of the four basic psychological needs. Let the group know how much time they have to get the job done. They are to list as many feelings as they can for their need, i.e., belonging: (1) connected, (2) loved, (3) secure. Have each group select a recorder, timekeeper, and reporter. The recorder writes down the group's ideas on the newsprint, the timekeeper keeps the group aware of elapsed time, and the reporter will report out to the community. Have each group report out. You may wish to post their work. Process their work by asking. How powerful are these needs? Would you do anything if your needs were not met? Do you do a better job at school if these needs are met? Can you see how these needs drive behavior?

# Day Two: Meeting Needs in the Classroom

## Preparation Required and Materials Needed

Meeting My Needs: Classroom Community Worksheet

## Lesson Directions

Divide your students into groups of four. Explain that each member is responsible for completing one section (one need) of the worksheet and specify how much time you are allowing for this part of the activity. After students have completed their section of the worksheet, allow time for them to explain and discuss their responses with their group members. Again, specify time. Ask for a couple of volunteers to compile individual group responses into one comprehensive list. The volunteer's job is to eliminate duplicates. This can be done as homework (split by particular needs), or during recess, homeroom, etc. The idea is that the volunteers support the Community by going the extra mile. Explain the dynamic to the whole class.

## Day Three: Meeting Needs in the Classroom

### Preparation Required and Materials Needed
None.

## Lesson Directions

Thank your volunteers. Lead the class in a discussion of the summary sheet responses. A student you wish to empower may lead the discussion. The objective is to eliminate any responses that do not meet the "adaptive/fair" criteria (adaptive: a reasonable chance of being successful; fair: safe for all involved and does not limit the rights of others to meet their needs). Naturally, common sense should prevail, and you may need to eliminate some responses. If so, remember to explain your thinking to your students.

Once again, ask for a volunteer. This time, you are looking for someone with good printing skills. The job is to create a visually pleasing summary list for each need. The lists can be displayed in the community. Again, you empower an individual to support their community this time with their special skill.

# Meeting My Needs: Classroom Community

In my Classroom Community, I can meet my need to

**Belong**: Be connected with other community members, be involved in community activities, be comfortable, and feel secure.

_____
_____
_____
_____
_____
_____
_____
_____
_____
_____
_____
_____

**Be competent**: Be successful, recognized, and able to control my outcomes.

_____
_____
_____
_____
_____
_____
_____
_____
_____
_____
_____
_____

# Meeting My Needs: Classroom Community

In my Classroom Community, I can meet my need to

**Be Independent:**, Make choices that matter, direct my own destiny, and enjoy some basic freedom.

_____
_____
_____
_____
_____
_____
_____
_____
_____
_____

**Have fun:** Experience, laughter, basic enjoyment, and down time.

_____
_____
_____
_____
_____
_____
_____
_____
_____

# Extending Activities

## Individual Behavior Analysis

Complete the "Individual Behavior Analysis" worksheet. This worksheet can be used proactively to promote introspection or as a behavior change tool. The worksheet is provided at the end of the chapter.

## Visual Representations

Art project, visual representation of each of the basic psychological needs.

## Needs Posters

Posters for each of the needs displayed prominently in your room (I got my need to be competent met when _____). Students are free to make an entry anytime they realize they are meeting a need. After several days, you have lists that can be used to revisit the concept of needs.

## Worksheet Needs and Behavior

Complete the "My Needs Drive My Behavior" Worksheet. The worksheet is provided at the end of the chapter.

## Walk and Talk

Do the Walk and Talk exercise. Have your students complete the worksheet and discuss the activity with their partners. You may wish to take this activity a step further and process with the whole group. The exercise is provided at the end of the chapter.

## Meeting My Needs in School/Outside of School

Complete the "Meeting My Needs: School Community" and/or the "Meeting My Needs: Outside of School" worksheets as individual seatwork or small group work. Process. Worksheets are provided at the end of the chapter.

# Individual Student Behavior Analysis

Name_____ Date:_____

Reason for completing this worksheet:
_____
_____
_____

Describe your behavior:
_____
_____
_____

I believe this behavior is an attempt to meet my need to (check all that apply)

    Belong____    Be Competent_____    Be Independent_____    Have Fun_____

Is my behavior adaptive? (reasonable chance of being successful)

    Yes_____    No_____

Is my behavior fair? (respectful of other Community member's rights)

    Yes_____    No_____

If you answered no to either question as a responsible Community member and a self directed individual, take a few minutes to write a plan for getting your need(s) met in an adaptive and fair manner.

Plan:
_____
_____
_____
_____
_____
_____
_____

Ask for help if you are stuck!

# Needs Drive My Behavior

Everything we do (our behavior) is done to help us meet a basic need. Some of the needs are the need to *belong*, to be *competent*, to be *independent*, and the need to have *nun*.

1. Choose one of these needs and enter it in the middle box of the figure below.
2. In the six boxes surrounding your need, fill in the behaviors it drives
3. In each box, circle (A) if the behavior is adaptive. Also circle (F) if the behavior is fair. The word *adaptive* means that that the behavior has a reasonable chance of helping you meet your need. The word *fair* means that the behavior is safe and does not limit the rights of others to meet their needs. Responsible community members meet their needs with behaviors that are adaptive and fair.

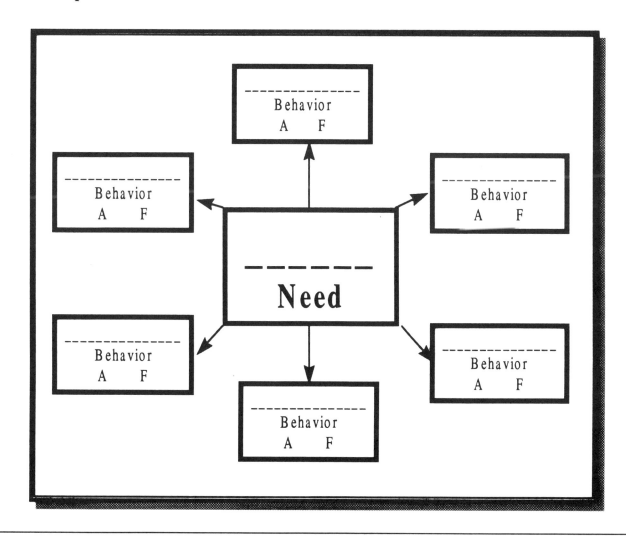

# Walk and Talk

*You need a partner to do this exercise. One partner puts on a blindfold, and the other partner leads the blindfolded partner around an area designated by the teacher. You may choose (with your partner's permission) to either hold your partner's hand and lead that person around, put a hand on one shoulder and guide that person around, or maintain no physical contact and direct your partner around verbally. When you finish your walk, get ready for the talk by completing this worksheet. Use one or two word responses.*

Blindfolded Partner: During our walk, I felt like this about my need for:

| Belonging | Competence | Independence | Fun |
|---|---|---|---|
| | | | |
| | | | |
| | | | |
| | | | |
| | | | |
| | | | |
| | | | |
| | | | |

Leader Partner: During our walk, I felt like this about my need for:

| Belonging | Competence | Independence | Fun |
|---|---|---|---|
| | | | |
| | | | |
| | | | |
| | | | |
| | | | |
| | | | |
| | | | |
| | | | |

Discuss your answers with your partner. Do they differ? If so why? Can you relate this experience to some everyday situations?

# Meeting My Needs: School Community

In my School Community, I can meet my need to

**Belong**: Be connected with schoolmates, be involved in social activities, be comfortable, and be secure.

_____
_____
_____
_____
_____
_____
_____
_____
_____
_____
_____

**Be competent:** Be successful, be recognized, and be able to control my outcomes.

_____
_____
_____
_____
_____
_____
_____
_____
_____
_____

# Meeting My Needs: School Community

In my School Community, I can meet my need to

**Be independent:** Make choices that matter, direct my own destiny, and enjoy some basic freedom.

_____
_____
_____
_____
_____
_____
_____
_____
_____
_____

**Have fun:** Experience laughter, basic enjoyment, down time.

_____
_____
_____
_____
_____
_____
_____

# Meeting My Needs: Outside of School

Outside of school, I can meet my need to

Belong, be connected with other people, be involved, be comfortable, feel secure, and feel safe.

_____
_____
_____
_____
_____
_____
_____
_____
_____
_____

Be competent, successful, recognized, and able to control my outcomes.

_____
_____
_____
_____
_____
_____
_____
_____
_____
_____

**Meeting My Needs: Outside of School, Page 2.**

# Meeting My Needs: Outside of School

Outside of school, I can meet my need to

Be Independent, make choices that matter, direct my own destiny, and enjoy some basic freedom.

_____
_____
_____
_____
_____
_____
_____
_____
_____
_____

Have fun, experience laughter, basic enjoyment, and down time.

_____
_____
_____
_____
_____
_____
_____
_____
_____
_____

# Chapter VII

# COMMUNICATION SKILLS

## Outcomes

1. Students will learn to use active listening.
2. Students will learn to use "I" Messages.
3. Students will learn how individual perspective affects individuals' opinions.
4. Students will learn to use the conflict resolution skills of brainstorming and finding mutual interests.

## Teacher Information

The Classroom Community Model is built on the premise that community members will both be invested in and capable of communicating effectively with each other. By helping community members to get to know each other, and by providing them opportunities to have fun with each other, to support each other, and to accept some responsibility for each other's success, the teacher nurtures students' desire to communicate honestly and effectively. Having a desire to do something and possessing the skills required to actually do it are two separate things. For too long, educators have refused to accept responsibility for teaching basic communication skills. Their refusal is often justified by arguments that these skills used to be and still should be taught and learned in the home. The fact is that many students arrive at school deficient in the communication skills necessary for their success not only in school but also in any structured group setting. A Classroom Community Model teacher accepts the responsibility and enjoys the challenge of teaching communication skills, as well as basic conflict resolution skills. Approximate instructional time for this component is seven (7) class periods

## Day One: Active Listening

### Preparation Required and Materials Needed

Review Active Listening Activities and decide if you will do one or more of them to demonstrate how important a skill Active Listening really is. If you choose to do the last activity, "Planning a Field Trip," you will need six plastic hats labeled with the communication stoppers. You will also need the Active Listening skill sheet.

# Lesson Directions

Explain the importance of being an active listener. Stress that active listeners:

- get all the information the first time
- seldom make mistakes and cause themselves extra work
- make friends easily
- do better in school and social situations
- are very productive in Classroom Community Meetings

Tell your students that active listening means concentrating on what the speaker is saying. It means blocking out distractions and thinking about what is being said. Suggested introductory activities include:

### Suggested activity: Classroom Disruption

Ask for a volunteer to tell the class about the most interesting/exciting thing that student did over summer vacation. Instruct the class to wave their hands and jump up and down in their seats to indicate they want to speak. Instruct several students to take a book out of their desk and start reading. Instruct a few more students to actually get up and start roaming around the room. Stop the activity after a minute or so, ask the volunteer how it felt to be interrupted. Open the topic up for discussion. Choose another volunteer and repeat the activity. This time, instruct the class to refuse to make eye contact. They may look down, look out the window, or focus on a hand held object such as a pen, pencil, or book

### Suggested Activity: Failure to Communicate in Small Groups

Have your students work in triads. Have students (A) tell students (B) and (C) about their favorite possession. Instruct students (B) and (C) not to make eye contact, not to nod their head, and not to indicate understanding verbally. Instruct them to whisper to each other and to snicker sort of secretively. After a few minutes stop the activity, switch roles and do it again. After all three students have had the opportunity to play both roles, hold a discussion, and ask if they felt they communicated much of anything. Ask the students how they felt when they attempted to communicate.

### Suggested Activity: Communication Stoppers

Select six students. The students should be volunteers. Have students move their chairs to the front of the room and have them form a circle. Tell the students that they are to pretend that they are in a real meeting and that their task is to plan the next field trip.

Then almost as an after thought say, "oh, you guys know each other well and are comfortable with each other. You see no need to use active listening. I am going to give each one of you a special hat to wear. It is important that no one looks at their own hat. The hat will tell your classmates how to communicate with you." Have six hats ready and labeled as follows:

1) Shake, rattle, and roll. (Move and squirm.)
2) Laugh at me.
3) Talk with your neighbor.
4) Talk over me.
5) Lecture me. (You know better than that.)
6) Do not make eye contact with me.

Note: plastic hats are used as they are easily disinfected and may be used over and over again. Hat labels are provided at the end of the chapter. Give the group ten to fifteen minutes to plan their field trip. Stop the activity and go around the circle asking each individual if they know what their hat says? Ask how they felt. Ask if they made any decisions based on the way their classmates responded to them. Ask the whole class if the planning group was successful. Identify the six communication stoppers. Ask the class if they know of additional stoppers. Ask how the group would have done if everyone used active listening. Now that you have demonstrated the need to learn the skill of active listening, teach it. Use the Active Listening Skill Sheet. Either make a transparency to show the whole class, copy the information on the chalkboard, or provide a copy for each pair of students. Assign your students in pairs, using a random selection method or, if you prefer, assign pairs that you know will work well together. Have students take turns practicing the skill through role plays. Some sample situations are provided with the skill sheet for your convenience. You may wish to write your own or have your students come up with situations they prefer to role play.

## Day Two: Conversation Traffic

## Preparation Required and Materials Needed

The green light handout. A Method for dividing the class into triads; count off by 3's, or another teacher-selected method.

## Lesson Directions

Ask your students what comes to mind when they hear the word "traffic." Share the following dictionary definition with them.

traffic\ 'traf-ik\ n 1: the movement (as of vehicles) along a route.

Discuss the definition with them. Tell them that you would like to ask them some questions about the definition: How do vehicles (cars, trucks, and busses) keep from running into each other? What would happen if vehicles did run into each other all the time? After processing several student responses, tell your students that you would like to share another dictionary definition with them.

traffic light n: an electrically operated visual signal for controlling traffic.

Explain that listening to them talk to each other, you think you have discovered a new type of traffic - Conversation Traffic. Tell them that you were so intrigued by the idea that you actually wrote your own definition and that you would like to share it with them. Share your definition of Conversation Traffic: conversation \ kan-var-'sa-shan \ n - traffic \ 'traf-ik \ n 1: the process by which thoughts travel from one person's mind to the mind of another person.

Ask your students: How do you think our conversation traffic is going? Do we ever have traffic jams? Do our thoughts ever crash into one another?

Suggest that you think you could use some traffic lights, traffic signals, and maybe even traffic laws to help with our conversation traffic. Tell them that you already wrote one conversation traffic law, the Law of Taking Turns or One Person Speaks at a Time. Explain that its just like a traffic light where cars from one direction (red light) stop and cars from the other direction (green light) go. Divide the class into triads and direct the triads to take turns with two students holding a conversation and one student serving as a conversation traffic police officer. Triads may choose a conversation topic of interest to them. The object is for the two students holding the conversation to take turns (one student speaks at a time). In order to help them do this, give each triad a copy of the Green Light - Go handout. Explain that only the student holding the Green Light may speak. The police officer will help them follow the law. Remind the triads to rotate their roles. Make sure that everyone has an opportunity to hold a conversation and to be the police officer, then process the activity. Suggested processing questions: Was it easy to take turns? Do we communicate better if we take turns? How important will it be to take turns when we hold group discussions, class meetings? Do we need Conversation Traffic police officers?

## Day Three: Practice Active Listening

## Preparation Required and Materials Needed

Active Listening Skill Sheet. Either copy the skill sheet on the chalkboard (large enough for all to see) or make a poster. Prepare one or two situations where you can demonstrate using Active Listening, i.e., your principal giving you some very important information, your doctor informing you of how to take a prescription, or one of your students asking for your help on an assignment. You will need a partner to demonstrate the skill. Invite your principal, another adult, or use one of your students to help you out.

## Lesson Directions

Revisit your conversation traffic lesson and reinforce how important it is for one person to talk at a time. Review the steps to Active Listening and do your demonstration. Process the demonstration with your class. Ask for volunteers to practice the skill in front of the class. Process their effort. Repeat with as many volunteers as time allows. Suggested processing questions: Ask the student who actually did the skill how that student feels about the success of the exercise. Ask if it was hard or easy. Ask the person who assisted if that person felt listened to. Ask how to tell whether the person was listening. Ask the class if all the steps were covered. You may choose to tell the class prior to the practice exercise that they will be asked if all the steps were covered.

# Day Four: "I" Messages

## Preparation Required and Materials Needed

The "I" Message worksheet provided at the end of the chapter.

## Lesson Directions

Explain to your students that they can never be wrong if they use "I" messages to express how they are feeling. Explain the difference between attributing your feeling state to someone else "you make me angry," and expressing/owning your own feelings, "I feel angry." Point out that an individual can certainly argue over the accuracy of the first statement, but that they should never receive a challenge on the second statement. Put a couple of sample "I" Messages on the chalkboard, i.e., I get very upset, I really feel happy. Have your students work in small groups, four to six per group. Give each group an "I" Message worksheet. Tell them to first list as many feelings (one word) as they can. Then ask them to write as many (feelings) "I" Messages as they can. Allow about fifteen minutes to have each group share their list with the class. Now link a behavior to a couple of the "I" (feelings) Messages, i.e., I get very upset when you call me names, I really feel happy when we get to play together. Have your students work in their small groups to add behaviors to their "I" Messages. Allow about fifteen minutes for the groups to complete their statements and have your students share their work with the whole class. Process the activity with the whole class. Some processing prompts are: Who really owns feelings? Does it help someone hear what you are saying if you use "I" Messages? Why? Does it help to link feelings with behaviors? Do you think "I" Messages could help us work out conflicts? How? Remember that empowering your students starts when you purposely teach a skill and culminates when you facilitate the use of the skill in a real life situation. Nelson, Lott, and Glenn (1993) suggest that "I" statements can be an effective intervention when communication breaks down. A student who has been taught the skill of using "I" statements and is now communicating in a blaming or judgmental manner should be reminded to use "I" statements. Your initial Conflict Resolution/Problem Solving community meetings will provide ample opportunities to reinforce the use of "I" statements. Note: "I" statements and "I" messages are used synonymously throughout the literature depending on the particular work and individual author.

## Day Five: Perspective Equals Opinion

## Preparation Required and Materials Needed

Carefully read the lesson, directions, and processing activity questions. Consider how individual perspective will affect your Classroom Community.

## Lesson Directions

Ask your students if they know what it means to have a point of view. Explain that someone who has a point of view on a particular subject has a particular way of looking at the subject. Use the following example to illustrate how important an individual's point of view is to how they judge something. A Potential Rain Storm:

- A farmer whose crops will die if the drought does not end soon
- A potential flood victim whose home and possessions may be lost if it rains one more time
- A boy who just received a new baseball glove for his birthday and who is waiting for his Dad to get home to play catch
- A girl who can not wait to wear the new raincoat and boots she received for her birthday
- A weather forecaster who predicted sunshine
- A weather forecaster who predicted rain

Process the activity by asking: Is anyone really right or wrong? Can you see how important someone's point of view or perspective is to decisions they make? Do you think this activity taught us any lessons we might apply to our Classroom Community? To problem solving? To conflict resolution?

# Day Six: Finding Mutual Interests

## Preparation Required and Materials Needed

Make a transparency of the "Mutual Interests Solve Problems" worksheet. Also make one copy for each small group. Decide on a method for dividing the class into groups of approximately six students.

## Lesson Directions

Tell your students that in order to use your Classroom Community Meetings to solve community and individual issues and problems, they must learn the skill of finding mutual interest, interests that the people in conflict have in common. Tell them that before you try to solve a conflict, you will practice finding mutual interests. Share an example or two demonstrating the concept of mutual interests. Two people who have been good friends for years but are now in conflict share the mutual interest of staying friends. Two students who want to listen to their own favorite radio station during homeroom share the mutual interest of liking music and in particular listening to the radio during homeroom. Give each group a "Mutual Interests Solve Problems" Worksheet and assign each group a different conflict from the Sample Conflict List. Allow twenty minutes for completion. Ask each group to select a recorder, reporter, and timekeeper. Have the reporters share their answers with the whole class. Process with the class. Processing prompts are: Was anyone in your group especially good at finding mutual interests? Could that person use that special skill to help our community? How? When? How difficult was this exercise?

# Day Seven Brainstorming

## Preparation Required and Materials Needed

Brainstorming is a basic problem-solving step. It is the process of listing all the possible solutions or ideas the group can come up with without engaging in evaluation. Experience has shown that children initially have a hard time not evaluating each idea as it is offered. Decide on a method for dividing the class into groups of approximately eight students. Make one copy per group of the "You Can Do That With This?" Worksheet.

## Lesson Directions

Tell your students that you have one more skill you want to teach them to make sure that they are ready to participate in community meetings. Ask if anyone knows what brainstorming is. Make sure they understand that when you brainstorm you will list any and all options without evaluating the options. Tell them that while this might sound simple, people new to brainstorming have a hard time not evaluating each option as it is proposed. Ask them if they would like to do an activity to learn how to brainstorm. Do the activity. Divide the class into groups of approximately eight students and tell the groups the challenge is to list all the uses for a particular community item, i.e.. a chair, a dictionary, a stapler, a trash can, etc. Provide each group a copy of the "You Can Do That With This?" Worksheet. You can choose to assign each group a different item, or the same item for all groups. Make sure your groups select a recorder and a reporter. A timekeeper is optional. Allow twenty minutes for completion. Have the group reporter report their ideas to the whole class. Process with your students. Processing prompts are: Was it difficult not to evaluate each use as it was proposed? Were you surprised at how many uses you came up with? How will brainstorming help us solve community problems? Was it fun?

# Communication Stopper Activity

Cut and tape to *Plastic Hats

| | |
|---|---|
| **Shake, rattle, and roll.**<br>**(Move and squirm)** | **Laugh at me.** |
| **Talk with your neighbor.** | **Talk over me.** |
| **Lecture me.**<br>**You know better than that.** | **Do not make eye contact.** |

*plastic hats can be wiped with a mild disinfectant between uses.

# GREEN LIGHT - - - - - GO

# Active Listening Skill Sheet

| **Skill Steps** | **Description** |
|---|---|
| 1. Look at the person who is talking. Make eye contact |  |
| 2. Stay still. This will help you concentrate and lets the other person know you are listening. |  |
| 3. Hear what is being said. Think about it. Nod your head. |  |
| 4. Summarize and repeat what was said; ask a question to clarify what was said; acknowledge your agreement by saying yes. |  |

---

Playground: A friend tells you the rules to a new game.

Classroom: Your teacher gives directions for an art project.

Field Trip: Your group leader tells you where to meet after lunch.

# "I" Messages Worksheet

**Feelings** ( one word answers) _____

_____  _____  _____  _____
_____  _____  _____  _____
_____  _____  _____  _____
_____  _____  _____  _____

## "I" Messages (fill in the blank)

| Feelings | Behaviors |
|---|---|
| I feel _____ | when _____ |
| I feel _____ | when _____ |
| I feel _____ | when _____ |
| I get _____ | when _____ |
| I get _____ | when _____ |
| I get _____ | when _____ |
| I felt _____ | when _____ |
| I felt _____ | when _____ |
| I felt _____ | when _____ |
| I felt _____ | when _____ |
| I felt _____ | when _____ |

# Mutual Interests Solve Problems

Briefly describe the conflict you will be working on

_____
_____
_____
_____

Briefly describe both points of view/individual perspective

_____
_____
_____
_____

Can you find areas of mutual interest upon which to build a resolution? List some here.

_____
_____
_____
_____

Group Members:

_____
_____

# Sample Conflicts

1) Two friends find out that they are both applying for the same job. Pete is trying to save money to buy a car. Sam is trying to earn enough money to pay his parents for his share of the family automobile insurance premium so that he can drive the family car.

2) Tyra and Amy are good friends. They have been friends for the last three years. They have a lot in common and do a lot together. Tyra is upset with Amy because she has learned that Amy is doing things with Joan, a new girl in their school. Tyra feels that Amy is not being a good friend. Amy feels that she is just being nice to the new girl. Amy also feels that Joan likes to do some things that Tyra does not.

3) Jerome and Fred are playing touch football at recess. They bump into each other hard and both get upset. They never really liked each other too much and end up calling each other names. They have to be separated by the recess monitor and are brought to the principal's office. The Principal tells them that fighting is usually a suspension, however, she will not suspend them if they can work the thing out themselves. If they don't, she will have to call their parents and write the suspensions. Jerome's mother works and his father is out of town. Fred's father is a single parent and looses money each time he has to miss work.

4) Mary and Latrice want to use the same resource book for their Classroom Community History project. They both are trying to meet the fast approaching deadline. Both girls are serious students. Mary wants to get an "A" and knows that she needs the book to do her best job. Latrice always gets "A's" and she believes the book is a necessary part of her project. Both girls consider themselves responsible community members.

## Commonly Found Common Interests

- Preservation of Friendship.

- Restoration of Friendship.

- Maintain position of responsibility in the Classroom Community.

- Maintain respect of friends, community members.

- Save face with friends, community members.

- Avoid sanctions, such as, calls to parents, parent conferences, in-school or out-of-school suspensions, detentions.

- Desire to solve the conflict within the Classroom Community - keep the power in the Community.

- Desire not to waste time off task, commitment to learning.

# You Can Do That With This?

**Item:** _____

**List the most common use for this item**
_____
_____


**Brainstorm your brains and list as many other uses as you can think of. 2, 3, 4, 5, 6, 7, 8, brains are better than 1.**

_____  _____
_____  _____
_____  _____
_____  _____
_____  _____
_____  _____
_____  _____
_____  _____
_____  _____
_____  _____
_____  _____
_____  _____

**Group Members**

_____  _____
_____  _____
_____  _____

# Extending Activities

## Tall Tale Big Problem

Quietly whisper the following rumor to one of your students and ask them to pass it on. Tell them it is very important that they pass it on and that they tell the person that they pass it on to how important it is that they pass it on. Sample rumor: The principal's dog died and the principal's husband was supposed to have the dog buried in the Heavenly Hounds Pet Cemetery. However, he is very cheap and he buried the doggy in the principal's backyard and the principal is having terrible nightmares. Do you think we should tell the principal about the dog? Once the rumor makes its rounds, asks the last person to recite the rumor for the class. Ask the first person to read the actual rumor. Lead discussion on rumors, on "he says -she says." The activity works best if you quietly whisper the rumor to the first student while the students are engaged in an individual seatwork activity.

## Take-A-Look Through My Glasses

Take-A-Look Through My Glasses --Explain to your students that we all have our own special glasses that we use to see things our special way. These glasses are sort of given to us by our parents, our relatives, our friends, and our experiences. Experiences include where we grow-up, what we like to do, places we go, how much money we have, our culture and its customs, etc. Provide your students a few concrete examples, such as if you are rich, $20.00 is not a lot of money for a birthday gift, but if money is tight in your family, $10.00 is a lot of money. If you grow up in Florida, are you as hot in 100• plus heat as if you grow up in Minnesota? If you are from a culture that says you show adults respect by not making eye contact, what happens when you are dealing with an adult who grew up in a culture where you show an adult respect by making direct eye contact? Take-A-Look Through My Glasses is a game that shows how important an individual's point of view (special glasses) is to how they figure out situations and decide how to behave. Play the game hard and you will learn how to put on your friends' glasses and take a look at how things look to them.

Ask for a student volunteer and explain that you will ask the student some questions and assign the student some tasks. Make sure to tell them that they will be wearing a magic pair of glasses (give them an actual pair of glasses) that transforms them into someone or something other than themselves. Tell them they must answer the questions and perform the task as they think the person or thing they have become would do.

| Roles | Questions/Tasks |
|---|---|
| Alligator<br>Elephant<br>Eagle<br>Physically Strong Person<br>Physically Weak Person<br>Old Person (80-90 yrs.)<br>Toddler (2-3 yrs.)<br>Blind Person<br>New Student<br>Teacher<br>Principal<br>Doctor<br>Football Player<br>Person (particular race)<br>Person (particular religion)<br>Person (tall, short, thin, heavy,)<br>Other_____ | What is your favorite thing to do for fun?<br>What is your least favorite chore?<br>Who is your best friend?<br>Who do you consider mean?<br>Where would your favorite place to live be?<br>What do you most like to eat?<br>When people put you down what do they say?<br>When do you feel (happy, sad, mad, nervous, relaxed, proud)?<br>Who is your hero?<br>Demonstrate making a free throw.<br>Demonstrate eating dinner.<br>Show us how you look/act when you are (happy, sad, mad, nervous, relaxed, proud).<br>Other_____ |

Variations - whisper the role to your volunteers. Have them do the exercise then have the class guess who/what they were. Another fun variation is to have the volunteers answer/perform first as themselves then as the assigned role.

Processing prompts for *Take-A-Look Through My Glasses* include: How important is a person's point of view? Is it helpful to consider the other person's point of view when trying to solve a conflict? How would considering each other's point of view help our community? Was it fun?

# Chapter VIII

# OUTCOMES

> *If you want to be important do important things*
> Motto PACE High School
> Community Service Program

## Outcomes

- Students will demonstrate an understanding of the cause and effect relationship between behavior and outcomes.
- Students will consider their abilities to control their own outcomes.
- Students will consider both positive and negative outcomes and the importance of accepting the responsibility for both.
- Students will write instructional outcomes in preparation for writing Responsibility Plans.

## Teacher Information

In order for your students to develop an internal locus of control and to take primary responsibility for how well they do in school and in life, they must understand the relationship between their behavior and the results of their behavior (often referred to as consequences or outcomes). Once they have an intellectual understanding of this relationship, you can support them in their attempts to accept ownership of and responsibility for their outcomes. It is important to note that some children, especially children that can be considered "at-risk," have difficulty accepting ownership not only of their negative outcomes but their positive outcomes as well. In this case, the child not only learns few constructive lessons from failures but also doesn't learn from successes. If this type of child fails a test, the child will project that failure (the teacher is a bad teacher and did not teach well, the test was a dumb test, the teacher did not grade fairly); conversely, if the child passes the test, the child will project the success (the teacher made the test too easy, they had lucky guesses, they were lucky and studied the right stuff). In either case, the child does very little, if any, internalizing. In the case of the failed test, the child sees no reason to change any behavior. It was the teacher's fault, and any change that needs to happen should be done by the teacher. In the case of the passed test, the child not only fails to identify the things done right so that future success can be built on identified successful behaviors, but maybe more importantly, the child fails to build self-esteem and an "I can" attitude. Good teachers do not assume that children automatically make connections between behavior and outcomes. They repeatedly present their students with evidence of the cause and effect relationship as it represents itself in daily life. They provide ample opportunities for their students to engage in guided and independent self-evaluation. They help students to create and visit artifacts of the cause and effect relationship, believing that it can be more dramatic and harder to dispute the cause and effect relationship if faced with a physical representation of the relationship at work. Representations of the cause and effect relationship at work in academic matters might look like completed study guides and outlines that support an "A" on a test, a completed goal/plan worksheet for passing a difficult test, or a look at the teacher's grade book, highlighting days absent, missing homework assignments, and incomplete study guides to support an "F" on a test. Representations of the relationship working in behavior/social matters might be reviewing a successful Responsibility Plan the student wrote to avoid being sent to the office, and actually sharing the teacher's referral log so the student can see in black and white the results of a great effort. You might even want to have the principal call the student down to the office so that someone really important can highlight and celebrate the student's success with a positive visit. If the plan was not successful, you would make the same visit to the referral log, this time paying special attention to anecdotal notes describing the specific behaviors that caused the referral to the office. In a well-developed Classroom Community, a meeting to allow community members to review the Responsibility Plan, provide the student feedback on their behavior, and constructive suggestions for change might be indicated. Often times, students listen better and hear more when the input is coming from their peers.

Students in a Classroom Community are expected to not only evaluate their own outcomes and help others to evaluate theirs, but also to write positive and negative outcomes as part of writing Classroom Community Contracts. Teachers should consider that most students tend to be overly punitive and very conventional in their first attempts at developing outcomes. Students usually begin by listing consequences (outcomes) such as detention, in-school suspension, and out-of-school suspension which are traditionally found in student discipline codes. Students pay little attention to logical outcomes such as loss of respect, loss of friends, lack of learning, and damage to community structure. In reality both types of outcomes are part of good Classroom Community Contracts.

Students should also be exposed to the concept of *Instructional Outcomes*. Instructional Outcomes are outcomes that do much more than punish — they teach. They are directly related to the rule and behavioral infraction. Instructional Outcomes help a student to solve the problem at hand, to right a relationship violated, and to once again assume the position of a responsible community member. This type of outcome can also teach new skills and inspire the motivation required to more effectively handle similar future situations.

An understanding of Instructional Outcomes and the ability to write them is important for students attempting to write Responsibility Plans (Chapter XI). Examples of Instructional Outcomes include:

- *Accepting the F (failure) on a test as an outcome of not studying, committing to study for the next test, completing a study skills packet, and/or taking a retest with the understanding that no matter how well I score my grade will not be over a C (average).*

- *Staying in from recess to do the homework I did not do last night so that I do not fall behind.*

- *Learning and practicing the skill of "joining in" so that I do not continue to have playground problems.*

- *Removing myself to "time-out" until I can rejoin my classmates without hurting their right to learn. Using my breathing/counting techniques to calm down.*

- *Practicing the skill of apologizing and then making the necessary apology.*

## Day One: Cause and Effect

## Preparation Required and Materials Needed.

You may wish to have a dictionary available so that you can have a student volunteer read the definition of the word *consequence*.

## Lesson Directions

Ask your students what a consequence is, and you might have someone tell you that it is what happens because you did something. Ask for an example of a consequence, and I bet you hear all negative consequences (detention, suspension, groundings, loss of privileges). See if you can prompt a positive example. Try these prompts: What happens when you study hard for a test? What happens if you work extra hours on your job? What happens if you really stick to a diet? What happens if you are kind and respectful to your classmates? Share the dictionary definition of consequence:

Consequence /ˈKan-se-Kwens/n 1: Result

Explain that a consequence is not positive or negative, but simply the result of an individual's or a group's behavior. It is what happens because you either did or did not do something. Tell your class that you know that the word consequence has a negative connotation. Most people assume a consequence to be bad. Tell your students that you would like to use the word outcome instead of consequence. Ask them if they can guess why. Tell them that you prefer "outcome" because it's easier for most people to think of outcomes as being either the positive or negative results of their behavior. Introduce the idea that we are responsible for all of our outcomes, both positive and negative. Close with student examples of personal behavior and the resulting outcomes.

# Day Two: Writing and Evaluating Outcomes

## Preparation Required and Materials Needed

Decide on a method for assigning small groups. Prepare a transparency of the "Outcomes: In bounds/Out Of Bounds" worksheet. You will also need one copy of the worksheet for each small group, and a copy of "Outcomes: Inbounds/Out of Bounds - Sample Rules" for yourself.

## Lesson Directions

Use a transparency of the worksheet "Outcomes: Inbounds/Out of Bounds" to teach your students to write and evaluate outcomes. Once you think they understand the process, have them work in small groups to complete the worksheet. Assign a different rule to each group. Allow about twenty minutes for completion. Have groups share their work with the whole class. Processing prompts are: Who can give me a definition of an outcome? Why do we use "outcome" instead of "consequence?" Who controls outcomes? Tell your students that they will have the opportunity to use their new skill of writing Instructional Outcomes when they learn about Responsibility Plans (Chapter XI).

# Outcomes: Inbounds/Out of Bounds

*<u>Instructional Outcomes</u> are related to the rule, reasonable in degree, fair in that they protect students' dignity, and productive in that they teach students how to do better.

Classroom Community Contract Rule:

_____

Following the rule = positive outcomes (list):
_____   _____   _____
_____   _____   _____

Not following the rule = negative outcomes (list):
_____   _____   _____
_____   _____   _____

Not following the rule can = *Instructional outcomes (list and evaluate):

| Outcomes | Related | Reasonable | Fair | Teaches | In |
|----------|---------|------------|------|---------|-----|
|          |         |            |      |         |     |
|          |         |            |      |         |     |
|          |         |            |      |         |     |
|          |         |            |      |         |     |
|          |         |            |      |         |     |
|          |         |            |      |         |     |

List Possible outcomes without evaluating them, then put an X in all the columns that your outcome meets. The In column is only Xed when you are able to X all four of the other columns.

# Outcomes: Inbounds/Out of Bounds
# Sample Rules

- Raise hand to be called on.

- Come prepared for class.

- Use other people's things only after asking.

- One person talks at a time.

- Keep hands and feet to ourselves.

- Call each other by our first names (we don't call each other names).

- Ask the person before we get mad.

- Use classroom voice (12" voice).

- Use "good" language (we don't swear, curse, etc.).

- Use rules taken from your Classroom Community Contracts.

# Extending Activities

## If - Then

Have students work in small groups to brainstorm

"if _____ then_____" statements.

## Essays

Have students write short essays on outcome related topics i.e. "I Earned Through Hard Work," "We Won Because We Prepared," "Failure And How It Happens," "Controlling Outcomes," "I Plan To Succeed By."

## Community Lunch

Celebrate by having a Community lunch. Decide on what you want to eat, one dish meals such as pizza, soups, stews, are easy to prepare and illustrate the idea of Community/group outcomes best. Everyone agrees to bring in one ingredient (you can have more than one student per ingredient). If everyone is responsible and brings in their ingredient, you have a complete dish. If not, you may end up with cheese pizza instead of cheese and sausage pizza. Do not get too serious with this activity. Your main objective is to have a nice community activity, but do point out that the outcome (the meal) is dependent upon the behavior (remembering your ingredient and bringing it to class). Also, point out that, because it is a community activity, the community outcome is dependent upon the behavior of each individual community member. Have fun with this one.

# Chapter IX

# COMMUNITY MEETINGS

*Meet to plan, meet to discuss, meet to solve, meet to celebrate, meet each other.*

## Outcomes

1. Students will apply their intra- and inter-personal skills to participate effectively in community meetings.
2. Students will effectively conduct community business.
3. Students will solve individual and community issues and problems.

## Teacher Information

The community meeting is, at its heart, the sincere attempt of a caring adult to communicate honestly with a special group of children. The importance of the classroom community meeting to the development of responsible students cannot be over-emphasized. Jones and Jones (1990) state that class meetings not only support the use of individual problem-solving conferences, but can also provide students with opportunities for improving their social and problem solving skills. Glasser (1993) explains that, although meetings appear to be time consuming, they are critical to the success of the classroom. Finally, Nelsen, Glenn and Lott (1992) believe that, without regularly scheduled class meetings, students don't develop the skills for success in solving a problem. The classroom community meeting is characterized by communication that is truthful yet caring. The old adage, "tell the truth, but tell it with love" is definitely applicable. The nature of communication in a community meeting is that of two-way communication. Rather than the teacher being the primary source of knowledge and thus accepting the role of knowledge giver, the teacher's role is one of facilitator. The teacher facilitates students' solving problems, confronting issues, resolving conflicts, and making decisions. Problems, issues, conflicts, and decisions are real. They are extracted from the fabric of daily Classroom Community life. The community meeting is not intended to be used solely on an as needed basis to solve the latest problem. It is a regularly scheduled part of life in a Classroom Community. Because it is used regularly and often, students are provided repeated opportunities to practice specific skills and become comfortable with their new responsibilities and roles as primary decision makers. The meetings provide a forum for the students' issues, concerns, ideas, and desires. While initially, most meeting agenda items will by necessity be teacher-generated, if working properly, the agenda will gradually become a student initiated agenda. Teachers should remember that in order to empower students, they must move from being "sages on the stage " to "guides on the side." How the agenda is formed is a teacher decision. Many teachers have their students deposit suggested agenda items in a classroom community meeting *agenda box*. This allows teachers to screen items that are better addressed individually and privately. Teachers must communicate not only the logistics of getting an item on the agenda but an open inviting desire to meet and problem solve with students about issues that are important to them. A welcome by-product of community meetings is that teachers will find that students are willing and able to hold discussion on an item that formerly would have demanded immediate attention. As soon as a teacher promises to place an item on the agenda for the next scheduled community meeting, the pressure is off, and the student has been validated. This provides the student with comfort in knowing that the teacher will honor all promises. I sometimes refer to this process as a "regulated permission" process. It supports the students' learning to accept and work within system oriented limits.

The community meeting is the hub around which everything else revolves. It is where students feel the power of being empowered. As discussed earlier, once you have put all the Classroom Community Model pieces in place, the weekly community meeting is where you work to pull all the pieces together. In addition to the regular weekly meeting the teacher always has the option of calling an additional meeting to address a pressing problem, an individual conflict, or to plan for an upcoming event. The teacher can always set a time limit for a special meeting. Students will get used to this limit and respect it.

Most teachers find that the open discussion format of the community meeting works best with the students sitting in a circle. Benefits to sitting in a circle include, 1) the circle is itself a symbol of community, 2) everyone can easily see everyone else, 3) the novelty of the circle indicates that the community meeting is something different, something special. Some teachers feel the disruption caused by moving student desks and furniture outweighs the benefits the circle configuration brings to the meeting. Some teachers work to minimize the disruption by allowing their students to experiment with various methods of forming the circle with a goal of finding the quickest and quietest formula. Deciding how to form a quicker, quieter circle can be a topic for a community meeting. I have seen all sorts of arrangements including making a circle of student desks, or student chairs, or simply sitting on the floor. I know of one classroom where each student has a small carpet square (samples from a local carpet shop), and when it is community meeting time, the kids just push their desks to the side and sit on their personal carpets. I have also seen some special classes where soft furniture and beanbags are used. My preference, when working in a traditional classroom with twenty to twenty-five students, is to take the time to form a circle for the regularly scheduled meetings and for lengthy special meetings. However, I always called a few special meetings of five to fifteen minutes over the course of a week. These meetings would be conducted with students remaining in traditional classroom rows. In this case, I felt the briefness of the meeting did not warrant the time it took to form a circle. Experiment and see what works best for your community. If you find your students are experiencing some difficulty taking turns speaking, get a nerf or tennis ball and make it a rule that only the person holding the ball can speak. I like to have students toss the ball to the next speaker; passing hand to hand really slows the discussion down. However, I stress that the speaker must have eye contact with the next speaker before tossing the ball underhanded. This is obviously a mechanical limit that should be discontinued as soon as possible.

There are two basic Classroom Community meeting formats: the community business format and the community conflict resolution/problem solving format. The business format is used to make routine community decisions and to plan for community events. The conflict resolution/problem solving format is used to address conflicts and problems between individuals and groups. Some teachers like to start every meeting with some kind of positive communication. Examples of positive communications are round robins, with every student having the opportunity to make a compliment to another student or share one thing they like about the community or share something about themselves, etc. Another meeting starting positive communication is to have one student volunteer to sing a song, share a favorite recorded song, read a poem, do a reading, or share a special object (trophy, toy, book, picture, etc.). My experience has been that starting meetings with positive communications works well initially. It helps to get things off to a good start; however, once your students become comfortable with the community meeting process, you may find the positive communications are steps you can do without. Instructional time for this component is approximately three (3) class periods.

## Community Business Format

### Steps

*1. Positive Communication (optional).

2. Define the task.

3. Brainstorm options.

4. Select an option and consider the effects on all involved.

5. Make a plan and act.

## Conflict Resolution/Problem Solving Format

Steps

*1. Positive Communication (optional)

2. Define the issue/conflict.

3. Look for win/win or mutual interest outcomes/options.

4. Brainstorm options - consider the effects on all involved

5. Select an option.

6. Write/Sign an Agreement.

* A positive communication may be used to start a community meeting. This is an individual teacher decision and is considered optional.

# Day One: Introduce Classroom Community Meetings

## Preparation Required and Materials Needed

Classroom Community Meeting Agenda Items List.

## Lesson Directions

Explain to your students that the Classroom Community meeting is a very special and important part of the Classroom Community. Explain that, unlike regular lessons, where the teacher has something specific to teach them, the Community meeting is different. In a Community meeting, we will all share our ideas to make important decisions regarding our community. We will plan activities, events, and special projects. We will work together to solve problems, confront issues, and resolve conflicts between community members. Tell your students that, so long as you can work together to take care of each other, the power will stay in your Community. Tell your students that you plan to have one regular Community meeting per week and that you can have additional meetings if something comes up that a meeting can address. Explain that they are expected to contribute items for your Community Meeting Agendas. Inform them of the procedure for getting their items added to the agenda and encourage them to do so. Lead a class discussion to brainstorm possible agenda items. See the Classroom Community Meeting Agenda Items List.

# Day Two: Community Business Format

## Preparation Required and Materials Needed

Review the "Community Meeting Agenda Item List." Make a transparency of the *Community Business Meeting Outline.* Also, make a copy of the outline for each student. Display the "Classroom Community Business Format Steps" on newsprint or the chalkboard where students can refer to them during their meeting. Decide on a meeting topic. You can use one from the list provided or choose one of your own.

## Lesson Directions

Present the Community Business format to your students using the transparency and ask them to use the outline you provided to take notes. Most teachers prefer to talk through a hypothetical meeting. Question your students for understanding and tell them it is time to hold your first Community Meeting.

If you decided to meet in a circle, now is the time to form one. Hopefully, you are at least going to give the circle a try. Begin your meeting by asking for a volunteer to work as the community's recorder. Explain that the recorder has several jobs:

1) List the meeting topic/task/problem.
2) List options/solutions developed through brainstorming.
3) Eliminate brainstorming options from the list as they are evaluated.
4) Indicate the selected options.
5) List any specifics as necessary.

Have your recorder take a place at the chalkboard and begin the meeting. Define the meeting's purpose or task and point to the Community Business Format Steps on the chalkboard or newsprint. The teacher usually has to take an active role in the initial meetings. Do so, but remember that your long-range goal is to facilitate, not dominate. Keep a focus for yourself of helping the kids to follow the basic format steps and reminding them to use their communication skills. Many teachers like to post the basic communication skills for easy reference. Make sure the kids experience some success and some fun. It is suggested that you hold at least three Community business format meetings before you teach and then attempt a Community conflict resolution format meeting. When choosing topics for your initial business format meetings, it is suggested that you seek ideas from your students and select topics that promise to lead to some fun and confidence. Examples include, planning a field trip, planning a community party, and developing a reinforcement menu. See Appendix C for reinforcement menu ideas.

# Day Three: Community Conflict Resolution/Problem Solving Format

## Preparation Required and Materials Needed

Review the Community Meeting Agenda Items List provided. Make a transparency of the Community Conflict Resolution/Problem Solving Outline provided. Also, make a copy of the outline for each student. Decide on a meeting topic. You can use one from the list provided or choose one of your own.

## Lesson Directions

Present the Community conflict resolution/problem solving format to your students using the transparency and ask them to use the outline you provided to take notes. Most teachers prefer to talk through a hypothetical meeting. Question your students for understanding and hold a simulated meeting using one of the conflicts from the Sample Conflicts List or one your students suggest. Use the services of a student recorder to:

1) List the conflict.
3) List areas of mutual interest.
3) List options/solutions.
4) Indicate selected options.

This format also requires the services of a second volunteer. The second volunteer serves as an agreement writer. The agreement writer works during the meeting to prepare an agreement based on the meeting's outcomes. The agreement writer shares the agreement with the students involved in the conflict and the Community. With the commitment of the students involved and the approval of the Community, the agreement is signed and witnessed. Some teachers feel this step is too formal. While there is some evidence that securing both signatures and public affirmations increases the likelihood that the agreement will be followed, this step may be omitted. Seeo Classroom Community Meeting: Conflict Resolution Steps provided at the end of the chapter for suggestions on conducting a conflict resolution meeting. Experience has shown that most students are capable of performing the recorder and agreement writing duties as young as ten years of age. Obviously teachers of primary age students must either perform these tasks themselves or provide additional support.

# Classroom Community Agenda Item List

- Develop a plan for forming a circle for Community Meetings.

- Plan a field trip.

- Plan a special culminating activity for an instructional unit.

- Develop instructional alternatives for learning the same curriculum.

- Plan an activity for parent teacher day.

- Plan a Classroom Community party.

- Plan holiday celebrations.

- Develop a Reinforcement Menu, a list of things students find enjoyable.

- Decide the qualities of a good friend.

- Decide the qualities of a good Classroom community member.

- Develop and write Classroom Community Contracts.

- Visit Community Contracts and amend as necessary.

- Develop and share goals.

- Develop a community service project.

- Resolve Classroom Community issues.

- Write individual and Community Responsibility Plans.

- Develop ways for the Community to support individuals attempting to successfully complete Responsibility Plans.

# Community Business Format: Outline

Steps

1. Define the task

   - _____
   - _____
   - _____
   - _____

2. Brainstorm Options

   - _____
   - _____
   - _____
   - _____
   - _____
   - _____
   - _____

3. Select an option (remember to consider the effects on everyone)

   _____
   _____
   _____

4. Make a plan-act

   - _____
   - _____
   - _____
   - _____
   - _____
   - _____

# Conflict Resolution/Problem Solving Format: Outline

Steps

1. Define the issue/conflict.
   - _____
   - _____
   - _____

2. Look for mutual interests or win/win options.
   - _____
   - _____
   - _____
   - _____

3. Brainstorm options considering the effects on everyone.
   - _____
   - _____
   - _____

4. Select an option.
   - _____
   - _____
   - _____

5. Write and sign an Agreement (optional).
   - _____
   - _____
   - _____
   - _____

# Classroom Community Meeting: Conflict Resolution Steps*

1. Define the issue: Give each disputant an opportunity to tell the community what happened.

2. Look for areas of mutual interest, (What do you want/need? What is most important to you? What will happen if you don't solve this?) If necessary, open the process up to the community at large. (What do you think these guys need to fix things? What interest do they have in common?)

3. Brainstorm options: Give each disputant the opportunity to offer possible solutions. (What could you do to fix things? What could the community do to help?) If necessary, open the process up to the Community at large. (How do they fix this? What are they missing?)

4. Select an option/solution, and evaluate its possible outcomes. (What are the outcomes for disputants? How does it square with Community Contracts? Are both parties' interests considered? Is it doable? Can we improve it? Should we role play it to test it out?) Have the disputants make the final selection.

5. Write and sign an agreement (optional).

\* from: Panico, A *Reaching Today's Youth* (Fall, 1997)

# Individual and Social Responsibility Agreement

Date:_____

As a Classroom Community member, I accept total responsibility for my behavior. I also realize that I influence the behavior of my fellow community members. I am a factor in their success and failures.

Participant Names

_____  _____

_____  _____

_____

Conflict Description

_____

_____

_____

_____

Participant Agrees To

_____

_____

_____

_____

Participant Agrees To

_____

_____

_____

_____

We have made this agreement because we wish to resolve our conflict in a responsible manner.

Participant _____ Participant _____ Witness _____

_____          _____
_____          _____

# Extending Activities

## Role Play

Role plays are great ways to have students examine conflictual situations. Ask your students to list some of the things that are regular sources of conflict. Write brief role play scenarios, act them out, and discuss them in a Community Meeting.

## Conversation Boards

Use the Classroom Community conversation board activity to get some conflicts to discuss and/or role play. Use a simple prompt like "Conflicts Look Like...," "Conflicts In Our Community Are...," "We Argue Over..."

## Daily Check-In Meetings

Consider having your students meet first thing every morning just to exchange greetings, share events and discuss the day's schedule. This can also be a time to see if a community member needs any special support. A check-in meeting can be as short as five to ten minutes.

# Chapter X

# GOALS

> *By every part of our nature we clasp things above us, one after another, not for the sake of remaining where we take hold, but that we may go higher.*
> -H.W. Beecher-

## Outcomes

1. Students will be able to set goals and write plans for reaching their goals.
2. Students will be able to evaluate goals and make adjustments to goals and/or activities.
3. Students will develop an understanding of how important goals are to a productive life.

## Teacher Information

Being able to set goals and develop plans for attaining these goals is a necessary life skill. Helping students to see the connection between planning and doing is necessary if we expect them to take control of their lives. Teaching students to evaluate along the way and, more importantly, to be flexible thinkers, capable of adjusting both goals and plans for goal attainment, will increase tolerance for frustration and tenacity for task completion. Repeated experiences in setting goals, developing plans, evaluating progress, and making necessary adjustments positions your students to develop an internal locus of control.

Most young people do not set goals. How many of your students do you think enter your classroom at the start of the school year with a plan? How many would you guess set any goals for the new school year? How many, if asked, could give you three specific things they intend to accomplish? How many could give you two? How many could give you just one? Helping your students to set goals and develop plans for their attainment will give direction to student behavior and establish behavior benchmarks to refer to when things start to fall apart. For example, when one of your students engages in irresponsible behavior, that student can be asked to evaluate that behavior in relationship to previously stated goals. Self evaluation is the best evaluation. Instructional time for this component is approximately five (5) class periods.

# Day One: Learning to Plan

## Preparation Required and Materials Needed

Mark off a two-foot square on the floor for each group of ten students. Masking tape works well.

## Lesson Directions

Tell your students that you have a problem and that you need their help. Tell them that the squares on the floor represent the size of the classroom the principal wants to give you next year. Explain that the principal thinks that you can fit ten students in that size room. Explain that if you are not able to do so that you will not have a job for next year. Divide the class into groups of ten and ask them to see if they can solve your problem. The challenge is to fit all ten group members inside the square. Once inside, all group members must be able to hold still for ten seconds. No part of their bodies can be outside of the square. Tell the groups that they have three minutes to figure out what they want to do. Give them five additional minutes to actually solve the problem, by getting inside the square. Process by asking: How did you decide what to do? Were you able to develop a plan? Who came up with the ideas? Did you stick to the plan? Was it fun?

Ask your students if any of them have ever set a goal, made a plan, and acted on the plan? How did things turn out? Try these prompts. Has anyone ever had to decide on a vacation destination? How did you figure out how to get there? Did anyone ever really want something and your parents said "OK, but we're not going to buy it for you?" How did you go about getting it? Has anyone ever really wanted to ask someone new out, but been a little nervous? What did you do? Where? When? In person/on the phone? Wrote a note? Go through a friend? Does anyone have a goal for today after school, no matter what the answer, even "I'm just going to hang out?" Use questioning to demonstrate that even "hanging out" is a goal. Ask (1) Where are you hanging out? (2) What are you going to do? (3) Who are you going to do it with? So: you are going to the playground to shoot hoops with Rick, Willie, and Tom. I bet you are actually going to try to win. I think you have a plan and maybe even a goal.

You should now be able to point out that we all set goals and make plans everyday; we just do it without much thought. Suggest that, if we really put our minds to it, we can do some big things. Wrap the lesson up by telling your students that you will be spending the next few days learning to set goals and make plans for achieving those goals.

# Day Two: Setting Goals and Making Plans

## Preparation Required and Materials Needed

"*My Goal Is*" worksheet. Either make an overhead of the worksheet or simply write the worksheet steps on the chalkboard or newsprint. You will also need a copy of the worksheet for each student. Think of a personal goal you can use to work through the worksheet with your students.

## Lesson Directions

Complete a "My Goal Is" worksheet using your personal goal as an example. Work through a second example using a goal one of your students shares. Have students complete the worksheet as individual seatwork. Ask them to work on a real goal (short term) something they can accomplish in no more than three days. Explain that you will review their worksheets after they have had a chance to act on their plan. Tell your students that it is very important that they only do steps 1, 2, and 3 of the Worksheet. Remember to allow three days between today and your next lesson.

# Day Three: Evaluating Outcomes and Adjusting Plans

## Preparation Required and Materials Needed

"*My Goal Is*" worksheets, with steps 1, 2, and 3 completed.

## Lesson Directions

Divide your class into groups of four students. Ask the groups to review their members' worksheets one at a time. After all students have shared their worksheets, the group should help those members whose plans were not successful to amend or write new plans as necessary. At this time, provide the groups a copy of the Goal Setting/Plan Writing Hints. Briefly review this handout and let the groups work. You may choose to process the small group work with the whole class.

# Day Four: Writing Individual Goals

## Preparation Required and Materials Needed

*"My Goal Is"* worksheet or eight index cards per student, depending on the instructional option you choose.

You may also wish to use Goal Setting/Plan Writing Hints and Individual and community suggested goals list resources. Some teachers like to make transparencies of these resources so that students may refer to them during the community meeting.

## Lesson Directions

Convene a community business meeting (format presented in chapter nine) to have your students write and publicly affirm three to four individual goals. Goals should cover both academic and behavioral/social concerns. You may use the My Goal Is Worksheet or simply have students write their goal on index cards. Index cards are durable and can be taped to the inside of a desk lid, the inside of a folder, etc. In any case, you want to have the goals available to use as a behavioral benchmark if needed. Some teachers keep a copy of student's goals to insure they are available when needed. This practice is highly recommended. You may choose to have your students hand write a copy for you or simply make yourself a photocopy.

## Day Five: Writing Community Goals

### Preparation Required and Materials Needed

Review the Individual and Community suggested Goal List and the Community Service Overview. You may want to make transparencies of these resources so that students can refer to them during the community meeting.

## Lesson Directions

Convene a community business meeting and have your students write and publicly affirm one or two community goals. Have an artistic student volunteer make a visual representation of your community goal(s) to be displayed for community members and visitors to see.

# My Goal Is

This Worksheet is a guide to help you identify a goal and write a plan for reaching that goal.

Goal: State your goal as clearly as possible:

_____
_____
_____
_____
_____

Plan: Be as specific as possible. Make your steps/activities small and easy to evaluate. List dates you will complete them.

_____
_____
_____
_____

Evaluation: Were you successful? Did you get close? Did you fail to reach the goal?

_____
_____
_____
_____

Plan Change: Be specific about the new steps/activities you will try.

_____
_____
_____

# Goal Setting/Plan Writing Hints

Before you go any further, ask yourself:

1. Did I stick to the plan I wrote?
2. Did I really try?

If not, you may want to do so before you adjust your plan or modify your goal. Ask yourself if your goal is realistic. Consider these questions:

1. Can I do anything to make it more realistic?
2. Could it be realistic at a later time?
3. Do I want to consider adjusting or changing my goal?

## Goal Attainment Resources to Consider

| | |
|---|---|
| ♦ Your knowledge | ♦ Your parents |
| ♦ Your intelligence | ♦ Your friends |
| ♦ Your physical strength | ♦ Your teachers |
| ♦ Your energy | ♦ Your counselor |
| ♦ Your spirit | ♦ Your church |
| ♦ Your commitment | ♦ Groups to which you belong |
| ♦ Your effort | ♦ Other |
| ♦ Your creativity | ♦ Other |

# Individual and Community Suggested Goals List

## Individual

Academic

- Pass all classes
- Earn Minimum of B's
- Complete all in class work
- Complete all homework
- Do all enrichment readings
- Do an extra book report
- Study for all general tests
- Other

Behavioral/Social

- Make and keep one new friend
- Ask before I assume
- No unexcused absences
- Keep out fights
- Address people by their 1st names
- No playground referrals
- Work as a peer tutor
- Watch hygiene, pay attention to dress
- Offer to help and do so
- Other

## Community

- All community members will pass the Constitution test.
- All community members will have their need to belong met.
- Our community will police the south lawn of the school and make sure it is clean.
- Our community will serve as peer tutors and recess monitors for the second grade classes.
- Our community will volunteer as readers for the local nursing home once a month.
- Our community will volunteer for Habitat For Humanity once a month.
- Other

## Community Service Overview

Meaningful Community Service Characteristics

- Students work with, not for, people/the community.

- Students' efforts have a real impact on individuals/the community.

- Students' work addresses real needs.

- Students meet and are encouraged to get to know the people they serve.

- Students have input into what type of community service they do.

- Students are provided the direction and time necessary to reflect (individually and as a group).

D. Davis (Summary of presentation, January 3, 1997)

# Extending Activities

## Public Affirmations

Students publish community and/or individual goals in classroom, school, community newsletter or newspapers. Students write letters to their parents affirming their goals. Students write letters to the principal, affirming their goals.

## Goal Partners

Have students choose a partner, or you can assign one, with whom they can share their individual goals. The partner suggests ways to insure goal attainment and looks for ways to be a special support for goal attainment. Reverse the roles.

## Parent Participation

Provide parents the opportunity to designate one goal they have for their child, and together, you and the student write a plan for achieving it.

# Chapter XI

# RESPONSIBILITY PLANS

> *Hold yourself responsible; first, foremost, and always.*

## Outcomes

1. Students will master the mechanics of writing Responsibility Plans.
2. Students will use Responsibility Plans to address individual and group behavior difficulties.

## Teacher Information

A responsibility plan is an individual plan a student writes when their irresponsible behavior is either significant in nature or frequency. The writing of a Responsibility Plan is not intended nor is it practical for the many, many minor problems that occur daily. The Responsibility Plan helps the student to self evaluate. It asks the student to accept responsibility for their behavior. It affirms that the student is responsible for their outcomes and the effect their behavior may have on their fellow community members. Most importantly by facilitating self evaluation you encourage the development of an internal locus of control.

Writing a Responsibility Plan is a process for doing things better. The student describes their behavior, identifies the community value and rule(s) that were violated, selects the basic need that motivated the behavior and crafts a simple plan to resolve the present situation and often times to also help the student handle similar situations in the future. Students write individual Instructional Outcomes for themselves. Some teachers find it helpful to revisit Chapter VIII outcomes at this time.

The Responsibility Plan may be written by the student, by the student with help from another student, by the student with help from the teacher or another adult or by the student with help from the community as a community meeting agenda item. Care should be taken to protect the student's privacy and thus their dignity. This means you must be aware of where you write the plan and always discuss involving other adults and/or students prior to doing so. Always ask the student for permission if you would like to involve another student or use a community meeting to write the plan. Unless the student's behavior is grossly disruptive to the community do not do so if permission is refused. If you still feel strongly that you must involve another student or the community share your reasoning with the student and tell the student that if they do not take control of their behavior you will be forced to proceed without their permission. Do so if the student does not respond positively. When writing a Responsibility Plan keep the following in mind:

- Attempt to have the student buy in, i.e., "Wouldn't you like a different outcome," "I believe you can handle this, would you like to try?" If the student will acknowledge a desire to change you are half the way there.

- Only help as much as you have to. The more the student does the more they learn. The greater gain towards an internal locus of control.

- The student must indicate the Classroom Community Value(s) and specific rule(s) they violated. If need be the student can be reminded that they participated in the writing of the Communities Contracts. The contracts are used as a behavior benchmark, a reference point upon which the student can focus to aid in their evaluation of their current behavior.

- The student must give a clear concise account of what they did. If need be the student may be questioned to secure an accurate account of what happened.

- The student should indicate the psychological need that motivated their actions. This can be difficult and students new to the procedure often need help.

- The student must square their behavior with their goals. Goals were written and saved and can be reviewed at this time. Goals are now used as a behavior benchmark.

- The student writes a plan to do better. The plan should be simple, concise, and doable. The plan is reviewed and revised as necessary until no longer needed. The first question to ask a student who is reviewing a failed plan is "Did you try?" If the answer is no secure a new commitment and let the student try again. If the answer is yes adjust/amend the plan and try again.

- The plan may include teaching a specific skill to the student, i.e., how to ask for help, how to negotiate, how to use anger control or relaxation techniques. It may include cues, i.e., the teacher addressing the student by their last name as soon as the teacher sees the student start to lose it. It could include the community promising to support the student's attempts to change by not laughing or otherwise encouraging the student's silly behavior. It could include using the community's problem solving or conflict resolution strategies - this could be done individually or with help from the group in a community meeting. It could incorporate a role play with the playground supervisor. It could provide a student seeking to meet a competency need a more acceptable behavior for doing so, i.e., the student becomes the community homework assignment recorder. A student who is attempting to meet a need to "Belong" may be helped to join scouts or the town's swim team, or children's theater group. A creative Responsibility Plan has no boundaries, why should it when the goal is to help a child/young person feel better and do better?

♦ Instructional time for this component is approximately two (2) class periods.

# Day One Understanding the Responsibility Plan

## Preparation Required and Materials Needed

Make a transparency of the blank Responsibility Plan form and the sample completed Responsibility Plan. There are several variations of the Responsibility Plan - choose the one you like. In the event you want to make your sample more germane to your particular class complete your own sample and make a transparency. Make a transparency of the I Need a Plan worksheet. Also make a copy for each of your students.

## Lesson Directions

Ask your students if they would like the responsibility of solving their own problems. Tell them that you want to give them the opportunity to do just that. Tell them that you are sure they are old enough and smart enough to handle the challenge. Explain that you want to teach them how to write Responsibility Plans -a plan for solving a problem or fixing a situation. Remind them that they already are becoming experts in this area. Ask if anyone can name some things you've studied or things you've done already that should be helpful in this area? You are hoping to hear - how to problem solve, how to handle conflicts, how to communicate, how to know what need is motivating me, learning to work together to figure things out, etc. If they do not tell you then you remind them. Put a Responsibility Plan transparency up and talk your students through the steps for writing a plan. You may want to use the blank form and fill it in as you go, or review a completed sample. Process the activity with your students. Some sample prompts include: How important is it that the student wants to solve the problem? Can you see how the Responsibility Plan gives you an opportunity to take control? Do you think there are some situations where writing the plan in a community meeting would be helpful? Do you think you can do this?

Assign the I Need a Plan worksheet for homework. The assignment is due tomorrow. Inform your students that their homework will be used to start tomorrow's lesson. Review the worksheet for understanding.

## Day Two Writing Responsibility Plans

### Preparation Required and Materials Needed

Method for forming small groups of from four to six students. Blank Responsibility Plans.

### Lesson Directions

Have your students use their homework, I Need a Plan Worksheets, hypothetical problems. Have your students write Responsibility Plans as a small group exercise. Check in with each group early in the exercise to make sure they understand the task and are off to a good start. Leave enough time to process the small group work with the class as a whole. Suggested processing questions are: Did the plans come easy? Did you have to stretch your brains? Do the plans you wrote have a good chance of success? Did it feel good to solve some problems?

## I Need a Plan

Name:_____ Date:_____

Some problems are little and we solve them without having to think very hard - I don't need a plan for them. Some problems are big and if not fixed quickly can get me into big trouble - I need a plan for them. Then there are problems that are not that big but they happen almost every day - I should have a plan for them.

Describe a big problem you sometimes have_____
_____
_____
_____
_____
_____
_____
_____
_____
_____

Describe a little problem that you have often_____
_____
_____
_____
_____
_____
_____
_____
_____
_____

Comments you wish to make_____
_____
_____
_____

# Responsibility Plan

Name:_____ Teacher:_____

Date:_____ Community: _____

Principle_____
_____

Rule(s)_____
_____
_____
_____

Behavior: What did you do? What were you doing?_____
_____
_____
_____
_____
_____
_____
_____
_____
_____

Option 1:

Responsibility Plan, Page 2

What need motivated your actions? _____
_____
_____
_____

Did your present behavior work? Does it have a reasonable chance of getting you what you want now and will it take you in the direction you want to go? _____
_____
_____
_____
_____

Plan _____
_____
_____
_____
_____
_____
_____

| _____ | _____ |
| :---: | :---: |
| Student | Date |
| _____ | _____ |
| Parent (optional) | Date |
| _____ | _____ |
| Teacher/Staff | Date |

Option 1:

## Sample Responsibility Plan

Name: _Harry_                    Teacher _Mrs. Smith_

Date: _8/17/01_                  Community: _Room 101_

Principle _All members of our community have a right to learn._

Rule(s) _Raise hand. Listen when the teacher is talking. Answer own question. Solve own problem. Ask learning partner._

Behavior: What did you do? What were you doing?
_Yelling out answers not waiting to be called on. Jumping up and down. I do this a lot._

What need motivated your actions? _Competency. I feel good when I get to answer._

Option 1

Sample Responsibility Plan, Page 2.

Did your present behavior work? Does it have a reasonable chance of getting you what you want now and will it take you in the direction you want to go?

_No. Instead my answers were not allowed (too bad I had most of them right). Other community members were aggravated when I did not stop. I had to time out myself. I ended up missing an important review._

Plan

_(1) Practice skill of raising hand (self talk) (2) Able to raise a closed fist 3X per day teacher will call on me first (3) assume responsibility for copying homework assignments on board nitely._

| Harry | 8 17 01 |
|---|---|
| Student | Date |

| | |
|---|---|
| Parent | Date |

| Mrs. Smith | 8 17 01 |
|---|---|
| Teacher/Staff | Date |

Option 1

# Responsibility Plan

*Protecting my rights is YOUR responsibility.*
*Protecting your rights is MY responsibility.*

Name_____
Date_____ Teacher_____

1. What was I doing?_____
   _____

2. Which value did you violate?_____

   1. the right to_____
   2. the right to_____
   3. the right to_____
   4. the right to_____
   5. the right to_____

3. Which need was I trying to meet?_____

   **Belonging**
   -being accepted
   -fitting in
   -being a part of a group
   -being cared about

   **Competency**
   -achievement
   -recognition
   -accomplishment
   -respect

   **Fun**
   -laughter
   -play
   -relaxation
   -enjoyment

   **Independence**
   -ability to make choices
      in my own life

4. Was this need met?_____

5. Did meeting this need the way that I did, violate the rights of another? If so, how?_____
   _____

Option 2

Responsibility Plan, Page 2.

6. My goals are: _____
_____
_____

7. Will this behavior help me or prevent me from reaching my goals?___
_____

*******************************PLAN*******************************

In order to meet my needs, to achieve my goals and to protect the rights of others, I plan to:

_____
_____
_____
_____
_____
_____
_____
_____
_____
_____

This is MY plan. I agree to review it and follow it daily.

| _____ | _____ |
| Student | Date |
| _____ | _____ |
| Teacher | Date |
| _____ | _____ |
| Dean | Date |

Option 2

# Quick Responsibility Plan

Name_____ Date_____ Community_____

**What was I doing?**

— Why? →

**Need that motivated me:**

+ ↓ −

**Evaluate the outcomes – now, later**

**Plan for the future:** ← Change

Option 3

# Responsibility Plan

Name_____

Date_____ Community_____

1. What was I doing?_____
   _____
   _____

2. What value did I violate?_____

3.   Which need was I trying to meet?_____

   **A. Belonging**              **B. Competency**
    -being accepted               -achievement
    -fitting in                   -recognition
    -being a part of a group      -accomplishment
    -being cared about            -respect

   **C. Fun**                    **D. Independence**
    -laughter                     -ability to make choices
    -play                            in my own life
    -relaxation                  **E. Freedom**
    -enjoyment                    -ability to make choices
                                     my own life

4.   Was this met without violating the rights of others _____
   _____
   _____
   _____

Option 4

Responsibility Plan, Page 2.

Plan:
_____
_____
_____
_____
_____
_____
_____
_____
_____
_____

Skills Needed To Be Successful:_____
_____
_____

Possible Positive Outcomes:_____
_____
_____
_____

I agree to try my best in following my plan.

_____          _____
         Student                              Date
_____          _____
         Teacher                              Date
_____          _____
          Dean                                Date

Option 4

# Responsibility Plan

| I wanted => 1 | I did => 2 |
|---|---|
| | |

| I got => 3 | I will => 4 |
|---|---|
| | |

Name_____Date_____

Supported by:_____Date_____

Option 5

## Responsibility Plans Take Hard Work

### Get Ready

- Sit down.

- Relax (use progressive relaxation/imagery/deep breathing).

- Commit to solving the problem.

- Hold yourself responsible and do it!

- You may have as much help as you need - your community will support you.

- Let us know what you need to be successful.

# Extending Activity

## Plan Writing

Write plans - evaluate plans. Write plans - evaluate plans. Practice makes perfect. Mix-up the activity having kids work alone, in small groups, in community meetings.

## Signs of Responsibility

Create some community signs that support students taking control, taking responsibility. The writing can be done in small groups and an individual from each group can publish the group's sign(s) on a computer publishing program. Kids love to see their work. See Appendix D for some examples.

# Appendix A

# ADDITIONAL TEACHER TOOLS

1. Role Play Situation Sheet

2. Discussion Challenge Sheet

3. Skill-Builder Worksheet

4. Reinforcement Menus

# Creating a Meaningful Reinforcement Menu

I. <u>People Reinforcers</u> (the peers or adults the child would like to spend time with or would like to have receive word of academic or other progress):

1. _____  2. _____
3. _____  4. _____
5. _____  6. _____
7. _____  8. _____
9. _____  10. _____
11. _____ 12. _____
13. _____ 14. _____
15. _____ 16. _____

II. <u>School Activity Reinforcers</u> (what the child would like to do in school):

1. _____  2. _____
3. _____  4. _____
5. _____  6. _____
7. _____  8. _____
9. _____  10. _____
11. _____ 12. _____
13. _____ 14. _____
15. _____ 16. _____
17. _____ 18. _____
19. _____ 20. _____

III. <u>Material Reinforcers</u> (the things the child does not own or have ready access to which they would like to have):

1. _____  2. _____
3. _____  4. _____
5. _____  6. _____
7. _____  8. _____
9. _____  10. _____
11. _____ 12. _____
13. _____ 14. _____

Appendix A *Additional Teacher Tools* **151**

IV. <u>Home Reinforcers</u> (people, activity, or material reinforcers that must be provided at home. You must have the complete cooperation of the parents):

1. _____    2. _____
3. _____    4. _____
5. _____    6. _____
7. _____    8. _____
9. _____    10. _____
11. _____   12. _____
13. _____   14. _____
15. _____   16. _____

V. <u>Creative Reinforcers</u> (anything you could not fit in categories I-IV):

1. _____    2. _____
3. _____    4. _____
5. _____    6. _____
7. _____    8. _____
9. _____    10. _____
11. _____   12. _____
13. _____   14. _____
15. _____   16. _____

# Creating a Meaningful Reinforcement Menu
# Sample: Elementary School

I.  People Reinforcers (the peers or adult, the child would like to spend time with or would have receive word of their progress):

1. Principal (possibly lunch)     2.  Friend(s)
3. Parent (note home)             4.  School Nurse
5. Librarian                      6.  Maintenance Person
7. Kindergarten teacher           8.  A coach
9. Social worker                  10. Counselor
11. _____                   12. _____
13. _____                   14. _____
15. _____                   16. _____

II. School Activity Reinforcers (what the child would like to do in school):

1.  Computer Time                 2.  Classroom Helper (Jobs) --
5.  Industrial Arts Time          6.  Special Field Trips
7.  Board Games/Free Reading      8.  Spelling Bee
9.  Fun Nights                    10. Video
11. Bulletin Boards               12. School Plays/Skits
13. Pizza Party                   14. Popcorn Party
15. _____                   16. _____
17. _____                   18. _____
19. _____                   20. _____

III. Material Reinforcers (the things the child not own or have ready access to which they would like to have):

1.  Popcorn, candy, snacks        2.  Borrow woodshop tools/home
3.  Music (tapes)                 4.  Student's picture posted
5.  Pencils, pens, folders        6.  Posters
7.  Certificates                  8.  Stickers
9.  Popcorn/pizza party           10. Fast food gift certificates
11. _____                   12. _____
13. _____                   14. _____

IV. <u>Home Reinforcers</u> (maybe people, activity, or material reinforcers however, they must be provided at home. You must have the complete cooperation of the parents):

| | | | |
|---|---|---|---|
| 1. | <u>Family Videos</u> | 2. | <u>Family Trips</u> |
| 3. | <u>Clothes</u> | 4. | <u>Money</u> |
| 5. | <u>Tickets (games, concerts)</u> | 6. | <u>Positive Note to Parent</u> |
| 7. | <u>Extended Curfew</u> | 8. | <u>Game of Choice with Parent</u> |
| 9. | <u>Special gym shoes</u> | 10. | <u>Rent Video Game</u> |
| 11. | <u>Television Time</u> | 12. | <u>Cassettes</u> |
| 13. | <u>McDonald's</u> | 14. | <u>More time with Mom/Dad</u> |
| 15. | _____ | 16. | _____ |

V. <u>Creative Reinforcers</u> (anything you could not fit in categories I-IV):

| | | | |
|---|---|---|---|
| 1. | <u>Principal's Wall of Fame</u> | 2. | <u>Front Office Helper</u> |
| 3. | <u>Free Quiz Pass</u> | 4. | <u>Bonus Points Towards Grade</u> |
| 5. | <u>No Homework Coupon</u> | 6. | <u>No Detention Coupon</u> |
| 7. | _____ | 8. | _____ |
| 9. | _____ | 10. | _____ |
| 11. | _____ | 12. | _____ |
| 13. | _____ | 14. | _____ |
| 15. | _____ | 16. | _____ |

# Creating a Meaningful Reinforcement Menu
# Sample: High School

I. People Reinforcers (the peers or adults the child would like to spend time with or would have receive word of their progress):

1. Principal
2. Teachers
3. Pro-Athlete
4. Boy/Girlfriend
5. Social Worker
6. Grandparents
7. Speech Teacher
8. Parents
9. Friend/Classmate
10. Coach
11. Athletic Director
12. Maintenance Person
13. Counselor
14. Dean
15. 
16. 
17. 
18. 

II. School Activity Reinforcers (what the child would like to do in school):

1. Breakfast/lunch with teacher
2. Pass Person
3. Games, Art Projects
4. After school dance/game (free)
5. Bulletin Boards
6. Use Library
7. P.A. Announcer
8. Field Trips
9. Use Overhead Projector
10. Computer Time
11. Use Board
12. Use Teacher's Text
13. Class Parties
14. Pizza for Lunch
15. Shadow Older Student
16. Help Maintenance
17. Go Out to Lunch
18. Run Errands
19. Help in Office
20. 

III. Material Reinforcers (the things the child does not own or have ready access to which they would like to have):

1. Certificates
2. Homework Pass
3. Food (Pass to Use at Lunch)
4. VCR Tape
5. Pens/Pencils/Folders (School Logo)
6. Free Time
7. Computer Banners
8. Signed Poster-Athlete/Rock Star
9. Books, Magazines, Posters
10. Calculators
11. Walkman (use)
12. Stickers
13. McDonald's gift certificates
14. Record store gift certificates
15. Mall gift certificates

IV.  Home Reinforcers (people, activity, or material reinforcers however, they must be provided at home. You must have the complete cooperation of the parents):

1.  Use Car
2.  Go to Game with Dad/Mom
3.  Phone Jack in Room
4.  Extend Curfew
5.  Discount Movie Tickets
6.  Restaurant Outing
7.  Miss Family Event
8.  Stay Home Alone
9.  Money
10. Excused From a Chore
11. Video (Watch with Family)
12. 
13. 
14. 
15. 
16. 

V.  Creative Reinforcers (anything you could not fit in categories I-IV):

1.  Drawing for Prizes
2.  Teach a Lesson
3.  Tokens for Video Store
4.  Tell Jokes to Class
5.  Another School's Activity
6.  Guest Speakers (student choice)
7.  Read to Younger Kids
8.  Teacher Exchange
9.  Earn Back Absence Days
10. Reduce Detention Time
11. 
12. 
13. 
14. 
15. 
16.

**Role Play: Situation Planning**

Name(s):_____
_____
Date:_____

Briefly describe the role play:_____
_____
_____
_____
_____

Be specific about where the role play takes:_____
_____
_____

Who the role play takes place with:_____
_____
_____

When the role play takes place:_____
_____

What will you say (key words, phrases):_____
_____
_____
_____

If you are practicing a specific skill ("I" statements, Active Listening) list it here:_____
_____

Anything else you think is important: _____
_____

DO THE ROLE PLAY

| **Role Play: Situation Planning Sample** | Name(s):_____ <br> _____ <br> Date: _____ |
|---|---|

Briefly describe the role play: *Two representatives from our community want to ask the prncipal to pay for our community to take a field trip to the local adventure camp group initiative course*

Be specific about where the role play takes place: *In the principal's office*

Who the role play takes place with: *Two community representatives and the principal*

When the role play happens: *Make an appointment for early a.m., before the principal has addressed too many problems.*

What will you say (key words, phrases) *The trip will: 1) build community  2) help us learn to work together  3) help us work on our problem solving skills  4) cost only $10.00 per student = total $210.00  5) Invite the principal to go with*

If you are practicing a specific skill ("I" statements, Active Listening) list it here: *Active listening*

Anything else you think is important *Be positive*

**DO THE ROLE PLAY**

# Discussion Challenge

Choose A: Reader/Recorder/Reporter

You have _____ minutes to discuss the topic and prepare to report out your answers to the community:

| Topic: |
|---|

| Define: | Answer |
|---|---|

- 
- 
- 
- 

| Make Real: |
|---|

- 
- 
- 
- 

| Consider: |
|---|

| Completed By: | Date: |
|---|---|

## Discussion Challenge

Choose A: Reader/Recorder/Reporter

You have __25__ minutes to discuss the topic and prepare to report out your answers to the community:

| Topic: The Importance of Goals |
|---|

| Define: | Answer |
|---|---|

- What is a goal?
- What is a short range goal?
- What is a long range goal?

| Make Real: |
|---|

- My most important short range goal is:
- My most important long range goal is:
- 
- 

| Consider: |
|---|

- Is there a relationship between my most important short range and long range goals?
- If not, do I have short range goals that do relate to my most important long range goal?
- 

Appendix A *Additional Teacher Tools*

# Skill-Builder

Use this exercise to figure out the building blocks (specific steps) to a skill of interest.

Skill: _____

Step #1 _____
_____
_____

Step #2 _____
_____
_____

Step #3 _____
_____
_____

Step #4 _____
_____
_____

Step #5 _____
_____
_____

When developing skill steps, ask yourself, *"What are the individual parts/steps that make up the skill? What is the logical order of the steps? Are there both thinking (deciding, planning, evaluating) and observable behavior steps (say, do)?"* List both. Try to divide the skill into logical steps. Try not to make so many specific steps that you confuse yourself. Only write more than five steps if you absolutely have to. Many skills will have only three or four steps. Let your own common sense be your guide.

# Skill Builder: Sample

Use this excercise to figure out the building blocks (specific Steps) to a skill of interest.

Skill: _Handling teasing_

Step #1: _Stop. count backwards from 5._

Step #2: _Consider choices: a. ignore the person(s)   b. walk away_
_c. Use an "I" message to say how you feel   d. ask for adult help_

Step #3: _Make a choice and do it._

Step #4: _If choice a doesn't work, try choice b._

Step #5: _____

When deciding skill steps, ask yourself, "what are the individual parts/steps that makeup the skill? What is the logical order of the steps? Are there both thinking (deciding, planning, evaluating) observable behavior steps (say, do)?" List both.

# Appendix B

# ASSESSMENTS

**1. Classroom Community Assessment: Student**

**2. Classroom Community Teacher: Self Assessment**

# Classroom Community Assessment: Student

**Please Do Your Best Job: Your Answers Will Be Used To Make Our Community A Better Place to Be**

Completed By:_____
_____
_____
_____
_____
_____
_____        Date: _____

## Physical Environment: Do I/we like our classroom?

Do you consider our classroom attractive? Does it remind you of you?_____
_____
_____
_____
_____
_____

Do you consider our classroom comfortable?_____
_____
_____
_____
_____
_____

Can I/we identify specific areas where I/we do specific things?_____
_____
_____
_____
_____

# Classroom Community Atmosphere: If a stranger visited my/our classroom would they know it was a Classroom Community without my/us telling them?

Are photos of community members displayed? How? Where? _____
_____
_____
_____

Are community conversation boards displayed/used? How? Where? _____
_____
_____
_____
_____

Are community art projects displayed? How Where? _____
_____
_____
_____
_____

Have I/we brought in things that represent life outside of school to be displayed? Have we used them to get to know each other better? _____
_____
_____
_____
_____

Are our Community Contracts posted? Do they look nice? Can they be read easily?
_____
_____
_____
_____

## Opportunities To Get To Know Each Other: People who know each other give each other the benefit of the doubt-they are invested in working things out.

Name a few things we did to help everyone get to know each other: _____
_____
_____
_____
_____

Do we do enough Experiential Education Activities (activities where we do something first, then talk about it after)? _____
_____
_____
_____
_____
_____

## Community Contracts: The Process is more important than the product.

Explain why we wrote Community Contracts. _____
_____
_____
_____
_____

How much did you participate in the contract writing? Do you feel that your input (thoughts/ideas) counted? _____
_____
_____
_____
_____

Do you think we talk about our contracts often enough? Do we change our contracts when it makes sense to do so? _____
_____
_____
_____
_____

Have we used our contracts to remind us of our community values? Have we used our contracts when we write Responsibility Plans? _____
_____
_____
_____
_____
_____
_____

## Responsibility Plans? A plan for doing it right.

I/we have written Responsibility Plans for the following reasons: _____
_____
_____
_____
_____
_____

When do you review your Responsibility Plans? _____
_____
_____
_____
_____
_____

## Classroom Community Meetings: It all happens here.

Do we have regularly scheduled meetings? Do you know how to get your items on the meeting agenda? _____
_____
_____
_____
_____

Do you feel that we have problem solving meetings when we need to? _____
_____
_____
_____
_____

## Community Skills: Remember communication skills are necessary for community meetings to work effectively.

Do you feel we spent enough time learning to communicate with each other? Do you feel confident using our basic communication skills? Is there a specific skill(s) you think we should practice? _____
_____
_____
_____
_____

Do you have a communication skill we did not study that you want to learn or feel our community needs to learn? _____
_____
_____
_____
_____
_____
_____
_____

## Basic Psychological Needs/Human Behavior: Share your knowledge. Belonging, Power, Freedom, Fun.

We learned about basic needs. Are there needs I need to re-teach? Are there things about needs that you do not understand? _____
_____
_____
_____
_____

## Setting Goals: If you do not decide where you want to go you will end up somewhere you do not want to be.

Do you feel comfortable setting goals and writing plans? Do we need to do more work on goals? _____
_____
_____
_____

Have you reviewed your goals as part of writing Responsibility Plans? _____
_____
_____
_____
_____
_____
_____

## Outcomes: Not positive or negative, but simply the result of my behavior.

How much control do you have over your individual outcomes? How much control over community outcomes? _____
_____
_____
_____
_____
_____

What is the best thing about our community? What is the worst? Is there anything else you think is important? _____
_____
_____
_____
_____
_____
_____

## Classroom Community Portrait (optional)

# Classroom Community Teacher: Self Assessment

**Completed By:**_____ **Date:**_____

## Suggestion
Complete on your own and then consider comparing with a colleague or supervisor.

### Physical Environment: Would I want to spend time here if I was not paid so much to do so?

Is my classroom attractive?

_____
_____
_____
_____
_____
_____

Is my classroom comfortable?

_____
_____
_____
_____
_____
_____

Have I identified specific areas for specific activities/behaviors?

_____
_____
_____
_____
_____
_____

# Classroom Community Atmosphere: If a stranger visited my classroom, would it be clear that this was a Classroom Community without my telling them?

Are photos of community members displayed? How? Where?

_____
_____
_____
_____
_____
_____

Is there a Community bulletin board? How is it used?

_____
_____
_____
_____
_____
_____

Are community art projects displayed? How? Where?

_____
_____
_____
_____
_____
_____

Have community members brought in artifacts of life outside of school to be displayed? Has sharing occurred as a result?

_____
_____
_____
_____
_____

Are visual representations of Community Contracts posted? Are they attractive? Are they easily read?

_____
_____
_____

## Opportunities To Get to Know Each Other: People who know each other give each other the benefit of the doubt - they are invested in working things out.

Have I provided repeated structured and unstructured opportunities for kids to get to know each other and to know me?

_____
_____
_____
_____
_____
_____
_____
_____
_____
_____

Have I made sure to provide experiential education activities to encourage sharing, getting to know each other, and understanding and tolerating individual and cultural differences?

_____
_____
_____
_____
_____
_____
_____
_____
_____
_____

# Community Contracts:
## The process is more important than the product.

Do my students understand the rationale for having Community Contracts?

Were my contracts written as a community project, insuring participation?

Are contracts revisited on a regular basis and amended as necessary?

Are contracts used as a behavior benchmark for individual students and the community when writing responsibility plans? How?
_____
_____
_____
_____
_____
_____
_____
_____
_____

## Responsibility Plans: A plan for doing it right.

Responsibility plans are written for the following reasons and by the following people:
_____
_____
_____
_____
_____
_____
_____

Responsibility plans are reviewed as follows:
_____
_____
_____
_____
_____

## Classroom Community Meetings: It all happens here.

Do I conduct regularly scheduled meetings? When? For what? How is the agenda created (remember the concept of regulated permission)?

_____
_____
_____
_____
_____

Are meetings called as needed? For what? Who can call them?

_____
_____
_____
_____
_____

## Communication Skills: Remember, communication skills are necessary for community meetings to work effectively.

Basic communication skills have been taught. Are there skills I need to re-teach the group or individuals?

_____
_____
_____
_____
_____

I have identified/the community has identified additional communication/social skills to support Community Contracts.

_____
_____
_____
_____
_____

## Basic Psychological Needs/Human Behavior: Share your knowledge.

Basic psychological needs have been taught. Are there needs and/or concepts I need to re-teach the group or individuals? Am I providing opportunities for kids to meet their needs?

_____
_____
_____
_____
_____

## Setting Goals: If you do not decide where you want to go, you will end up somewhere you do not want to be.

I have taught basic goal setting strategies and have facilitated the setting of individual and community goals.

_____
_____
_____
_____

Goals are used as behavior benchmarks for individual and group Responsibility Plans.

_____
_____
_____
_____

## Outcomes: Simply the result of my behavior.

I have taught Outcomes and have facilitated my students accepting and internalizing the outcomes of their behavior. How?

_____
_____
_____
_____

## Thoughts/Considerations/Plans: What you think is important.

_____
_____
_____

# Appendix C

# PUBLIC RELATIONS

**1. Sample Parent/Guardian/PTO Letter**

**2. Sample Principal Letter**

# Parent Letter

Dear Parent/Guardian/PTO:

This year, our class will become a Classroom Community, a community where kindness, mutual respect, responsibility, and hard work will prosper. We will be learning communication skills, decision making skills, and conflict resolution skills. We will be writing Classroom Community contracts or agreements on what we value, rules to support the values, and outcomes to support the rules. We will be learning not *what* to think but *how* to think. We will have some responsibility for making decisions concerning our community.

Every week, we intend to hold a Classroom Community Meeting. This is where we will make decisions, practice our communication skills, and solve our conflicts. We think the best way to learn is to learn by doing. What do you think?

Sincerely,

cc: Principal

Principal _____

This year, our class will become a Classroom Community, a community where kindness, mutual respect, responsibility, and hard work will prosper. We will be studying communication skills, decision making skills, and non-violent conflict resolution skills. We want to handle as many of our own problems as is possible. We do, however, want to be able to call on you when we really need you.

We will be writing Classroom Community contracts, or agreements on what we value, rules to support the values, and outcomes to support the rules. We will be learning not what to think but how to think.

Every week, we will be holding a Classroom Community Meeting. This is where we will make decisions, practice our communication skills, and solve our conflicts. With us handling most of our own discipline, you should have some extra time to do those things you never have a chance to get to. Once we have things up and running, we will invite you in to check us out.

We will keep you informed.

Sincerely,

# Appendix D

# CLASSROOM DISPLAYS THAT PROMOTE COMMUNITY CONCEPTS

1. Benefit of the doubt is what it's all about.

2. Do the little things on a daily basis and the big things will come.

3. Hold yourself responsible and everything else will follow.

4. The really important lessons you teach by example.

5. To always be the best is impossible. To always be your best is awesome.

6. Classroom Community Meetings.

7. Do what's right for your students. You know what that is and you know how to do it.

> The really important lessons you teach by example
>
> — A. P. Panico

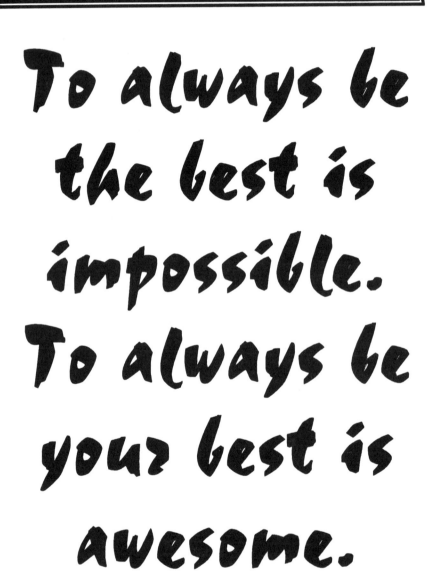

# Classroom Community Meetings

**NO DEPOSIT - NO RETURN**

We only get out what we put in

# PARTICIPATE!

*A. P. Panico*

> Do what's right for your students. You know what that is and you know how to do it.
>
> A.P. Panico

# References

Anonymous. *Not such a silly goose*. Workshop handout.

Beecher, H.W. in: Brown, H., and Spizman, R. (1996). *A hero in every heart*. Nashville: Nelson Publishers.

Chamey, R.S. (1993). *Teaching children to care: Management in the re... classroom*. Greenfield, Massachusetts: Northeast Foundation for ...

Curwin, R., and Mendler, A. (1998). *Discipline with dignity*. Alexan... Association for Supervision and Curriculum Development.

Edleman-Wright, M. (1993). *The Measure of our success: A letter to my c... yours*. New York, N.Y.: Harper Collins, Publishers, Inc.

Gathercoal, F. (1991). *Judicious discipline*. Davis, California: Caddo Gap Pres...

Glasser, W. (1969). *Schools without failure*. New York: Harper and Row.

Ginott, H. (1972). *Teacher and child: A book for parents and teachers*. New York: Macmillan.

Jensen, E. (1988). *Super-teaching*. Del Mar, California: Turning Point for Teachers.

Johnson, D., Johnson, R., and Holubec E. (1994). *The nuts and bolts of cooperative learning*. Edina, Minnesota: Interaction Book Company.

Jones, L., and Jones, S. (1990). *Comprehensive classroom management: Motivating and managing students*. Needham Heights, Massachusetts: Allyn and Bacon.

Markham, E. in: Brendtro, L., Brokenleg, M, and Van Bockern (1990). *Reclaiming youth at risk: Our hope for the future*. Bloomington, Indiana: National Education Service.

Maslow, A. (1954). *The farther reaches of human nature*. New York: Viking.

Nelsen, J., Glenn, S., and Lott, L. (1993). *Positive discipline in the classroom*. Rocldin, California: Prima Publishing.

Panico, A. Reaching Today's Youth. *The Community Circle of Caring Journal*, Vol 2, Issue 1, Pages 37-40, National Education Service, Bloomington, IN

Schrupf, F., Crawford, D., and Usadel, H. (1991). *Peer mediation: Conflict resolution in schools*. Champaign, Illinois: Research Press.

Driving Hawk-Sneve, V. in: Brendtro, L., Brokenleg, M, and Van Beckern (1990). *Reclaiming youth at risk: Our hope for the future*. Bloomingon, Indiana: National Education Service.

Wood, M., and Long, N. (1991). *Life space intervention: Talking with children and youth in crisis*. Austin, Texas: Pro-Ed, Inc.